WHY DOGS EAT POOP

Gross
but True Things
You Never Knew
About Animals

Francesca Gould
&
David Haviland

ILLUSTRATED BY
JP Coovert

G. P. Putnam's Sons
An Imprint of Penguin Group (USA) Inc.

Also by Francesca Gould

Why You Shouldn't Eat Your Boogers:

Gross but True Things You Don't Want to Know
About Your Body

For Mum

G. P. PUTNAM'S SONS
An imprint of Penguin Young Readers Group
Published by The Penguin Group
Penguin Group (USA) Inc., 375 Hudson Street, New York, NY 10014, USA

USA | Canada | UK | Ireland | Australia | New Zealand | India | South Africa | China
Penguin Books Ltd, Registered Offices: 80 Strand, London WC2R 0RL, England
For more information about the Penguin Group, visit penguin.com

Library of Congress Cataloging-in-Publication Data
Gould, Francesca.
Why dogs eat poop : gross but true things you never knew about animals / Francesca Gould and
David Haviland ; illustrated by J. P. Coovert.
pages cm
Audience: 8–12.
Audience: Grade 4 to 6.
1. Animals—Miscellanea—Juvenile literature. 2. Animal behavior—Juvenile literature. I. Haviland,
David. II. Coovert, J. P., illustrator. III. Title. QL50.G693 2013   591.5—dc23   2012051012

Published simultaneously in Canada. Printed in the United States of America.
ISBN 978-0-399-16530-6

1 3 5 7 9 10 8 6 4 2

Design by Marikka Tamura. Text set in Diverda Serif.
The publisher does not have any control over and does not assume any responsibility
for author or third-party websites or their content.

Contents

Coming up....

birds
drink
blood

1
Amazing Animals

Which Octopus Is an Expert Impressionist?

There's a species of octopus that can mimic an incredible range of other sea life. It's a small, brown-and-white-mottled mollusk called the mimic octopus, which is about 2 feet (61 cm) long, and found in waters around Indonesia. It can change its color and shape to resemble much of the local fauna. Many types of octopus can change color, and some are even believed to be able to mimic one other species, but the mimic octopus is the first known animal of any kind that can morph into a number of different physical impersonations in this way.

It can mimic at least 15 other species, including sea snakes, lionfish, flatfish, sole fish, brittle stars, giant crabs, sea stars, stingrays, flounders, jellyfish, sea anemones, and mantis shrimps. For example, it impersonates a sea snake by stuffing seven of its arms into a hole and waving the remaining one in the water. It impersonates lionfish by hovering above the ocean floor with its arms spread out, trailing from its body, just like the lionfish's poisonous fins. Its impression of a sole consists of building up speed through jet propulsion and drawing its arms in so that its body forms a flat wedge that undulates just like the flat body of a sole.

This talent seems to be useful in two particular ways. First, the mimic octopus uses this skill to get closer to its prey. For example, it will pretend to be a female crab to get closer to an amorous male crab, which it will then grab and eat. It also uses mimicry to scare off its predators. Most of the species it mimics are poisonous, and the octopus can tailor its impressions to the intended audience, ensuring that it mimics the creature that will be most likely to discourage or scare off the predator. For example, when approached by a damselfish, a mimic octopus will suddenly appear to turn into a banded sea snake, which is a known predator of damselfish.

If You Cut an Earthworm in Half, Do You End Up with Two Worms?

No. If you cut an earthworm in half, all you will usually end up with is two halves of a dead worm. Like most creatures, an earthworm cut in half will probably die. The only way it might survive is if the cut is made behind the thickest part of the worm, which is called the saddle, where all its major organs are found. If all these organs are retained, the worm may survive, but it will still just be one worm.

There is one type of worm, though, that will form two new worms if cut in half. A planarian is a flatworm that is found in many parts of the world, in salt water and fresh water and on land. Amazingly, a planarian can be cut across its width or its length, and both halves will regenerate as a living worm. This is

> a planarian worm can be **cut across** its width or its length, and both **halves** will **regenerate** as a living worm

possible because flatworms have very simple body structures, with none of the complex organs that an earthworm requires to survive.

Which Bird Drinks Blood ?

The Galápagos Islands are very dry, with a lack of fresh water. Birds need water in their diet, so the vampire finch has found a number of ways to quench its thirst. First, it drinks nectar from the flowers of the Galápagos prickly pear. Second, it steals eggs, rolling them from their nests and smashing them to drink the nourishing yolk inside.

The vampire finch's third method is even more extraordinary: it drinks the blood of other birds, usually masked boobies and red-footed boobies. It does this by pecking the skin in front of the bird's tail until it bleeds. Surprisingly, the boobies don't seem to mind being pecked and offer little resistance. Some believe that this behavior may have evolved from an earlier mutually beneficial habit of picking parasites from the boobies' skin. Over time, the finches may have inadvertently begun to draw blood and continued the practice as the nutritious blood became a key source of protein and liquid.

There is another type of bird, the oxpecker, that does something similar. Oxpeckers are found in Africa and feed exclusively on the backs and necks of large mammals, including cattle, rhinos, buffalo, antelopes, impalas, and giraffes. It used to be thought that oxpeckers enjoyed a mutually beneficial relationship with their hosts: the theory was that the oxpeckers cleaned the large mammals' skin by pecking away ticks, botfly larvae, and other parasites, often from hard-to-reach spots such as inside the animals' nostrils or ears.

> oxpeckers reopen **wounds** and feed on the other animals' **blood**

However, recent research suggests that, like vampire finches, oxpeckers may simply be parasites that perhaps once helped clean their hosts but now subsist chiefly by reopening wounds and feeding on the animals' blood. Oxpeckers do remove some ticks and larvae from their hosts, yet evidence indicates that they may not remove enough of them to make any meaningful difference.

Which Creature Builds Itself a Refrigerator?

Many mammals that live in cold climates are forced to hibernate in winter because a lack of available food requires them to conserve as much heat and energy as possible. But beavers have an amazing way of surviving the winter without having to sleep through it and miss out on all the fun. They build themselves an underwater refrigerated pantry, which provides them with a constant supply of fresh, nutritious food throughout the winter, even when the woods around them are barren and covered with snow.

When setting up home for the first time, a pair of beavers will choose a valley with a small stream running through it and build a dam. Beavers are big, powerful creatures that can grow to 4 feet (1.2 m) in length and have enormous, sharp teeth. With these, they cut down trees and drag them into place on the streambed. This construction is supported with rocks and then plastered with mud on the upstream side. On the downstream side, more tree trunks are laid lengthwise up against the dam wall to provide support against the increasing weight of the water. Gradually, the lake behind the dam begins to swell, so the beavers respond by lengthening the dam. As this process continues, they may use up all the nearby trees and have to travel long distances to find more. Beavers sometimes even build canals to transport wood down to their dam. A pair of beavers may maintain their dam for years, with some dams eventually becoming more than 100 yards (91.4 m) long.

Once the dam is built, the beavers start work on their underground lodge, where they will spend the winter. This will either be on the edge of the lake or preferably on an island for added security. The beavers build a tunnel that opens on the surface of the island and leads down to a second, underwater entrance. They cover the land entrance with rocks, branches, and mud and then excavate the inside of the mound, creating a large, hollow chamber. They are now extremely safe since their underground chamber is secure from above and they can slip into the water unseen.

When autumn comes, the beavers start to fill their pantry for the winter. They collect leafy branches and submerge them in the lake, where the near-freezing water will keep them fresh and green. As the temperature drops, the roof of the beavers' lodge freezes solid, making it practically impenetrable, and their food stays fresh safely at the bottom of the lake.

Which Insects Are
Used for Cleaning Museums ?

This sounds like a mistake. Surely you clean museums *of* insects, not *with* them? Nonetheless, there is a type of beetle that museum curators find extremely useful. The dermestid beetle eats dead skin, flesh, and hair, and one single beetle can strip the skin off a dead animal in just a few hours, leaving a perfect, pristine skeleton. Natural history museums use the amazing nibblers to clean animal bones that are to be used as exhibits. They are used by taxidermists for similar purposes.

Dermestid beetles can also be used by the police to help calculate how long a body has been dead, in a science called forensic entomology. Investigators generally focus on flies and maggots, which are usually

> **one single beetle** can strip the skin off a **dead animal** in **just a few hours,** leaving a perfect, **pristine skeleton**

the first on the scene; but if a body has been left to decay for some time, the presence of beetles is also a useful indicator. Dermestid beetles will appear during the final stages of decomposition to feed on the dried skin, tendon, and bone left behind by the earlier scavengers. Dermestids usually appear around five to 11 days after death.

In addition to preying on the dead, dermestids have a tendency to annoy the living. They are omnivores that love to eat grain, and they cause millions of dollars' worth of crop damage every year, making them a major irritation for farmers. They can also cause havoc in your home if you're unlucky enough to become infested. Let a dermestid beetle into your home, and it will munch your carpet right down to the bare floorboards.

Which Reptile Solves Crimes ?

Snapping turtles, freshwater turtles that are found in the Americas, mainly like to eat rotting meat, and they have a particular talent for sniffing out dead carcasses in the water. This ability has led police to use snapping turtles to help them find human corpses underwater. According to reports, the police simply tie a line to the turtle, and it leads them straight to the body. There are two species: the enormous alligator snapping turtle, which can weigh over 200 pounds (about 90 kg), and the common snapping turtle, which is smaller, rarely weighing more than 60 pounds (27 kg). Both species have large heads, which cannot be withdrawn into their small shells. They have very strong jaws and mobile necks, and will bite aggressively if threatened.

Do Birds Have Accents

A bird's ability to sing is partly inherited and partly taught by its parents. Scientists have demonstrated this by conducting tests on chaffinch chicks. If the chicks are reared in silence, they will still attempt to sing, but their calls will be only barely recognizable as a chaffinch call. They have to hear their parents sing before they are able to produce the full range and subtleties of the usual chaffinch song.

Since these songs are passed down through the generations, we might therefore imagine that birds in different regions would develop distinctions, regional accents. And this turns out to be true. Experts can recognize the different accents of chaffinches from northern England compared with those from the south.

In the nineteenth century, Australian settlers imported many plant and animal species from Europe to make them feel more at home in their strange new land. These included a range of songbirds such as blackbirds, which were not indigenous to Australia. Today, little more than a century later, the descendants of those blackbirds have developed a distinctive Australian accent.

blackbirds have developed a distinctive Australian accent

What Is a Remote-Control Cockroach?

Cockroaches may be unpleasant, but they are also remarkable creatures, and we can learn a great deal from them. Scientists love cockroaches because they're great for experimenting on. The nerve cells in their brains are quite similar to ours, and they also grow tumors that are like those of humans. As a result, scientists use cockroaches to study cancer, heart disease, and even the inner workings of the brain.

In one fascinating experiment, scientists at the University of Tokyo found that they could remove a cockroach's wings, insert tiny electrodes into its antennae, and use these to "drive" it via remote control, making it stop, go, and turn left and right. To power the electrodes, the cockroaches were also fitted with tiny backpacks containing batteries.

Now, this experiment may sound frivolous, but it could have valuable applications. Scientists are looking into the possibility of using remote-

control cockroaches in rescue work. With tiny cameras
on their backs, cockroaches
could be very useful in ex-
ploring collapsed buildings
and other dangerous, inac-
cessible locations.

> with tiny **cameras** on their backs, **cockroaches** could be very useful

In fact, cockroaches are not the only creatures to have been experimented on in this way. In recent years, scientists have carried out similar tests on remote-control rats, pigeons, and sharks. In theory, remote-control animals such as these could have numerous useful applications, including military surveillance, clearing land mines, or mapping underground areas. The advantage of using real animals in this way rather than building robots is that these animals can already deal with problems such as walking, turning, climbing, and avoiding obstacles, which turn out to be very difficult for real robots to accomplish, at least at present.

Who Was the Last Known Speaker of the Ature Language

The language of the Atures people of Venezuela died out during the nineteenth century. The German explorer and geographer Alexander von Humboldt was lucky enough to meet the very last speaker of this language while trekking through the Venezuelan jungle. During his expedition, von Humboldt made many fascinating discoveries, including the electric eel, the Brazil nut, and a previously undiscovered ocean current off the west coast of South America. Still, he had not managed to discover a single word of the Ature language.

Then, while visiting the neighboring tribe of Maypures, he finally made a breakthrough. He was led by torchlight through the remote village to the cage of a talking parrot. The Maypures explained that this bird had been captured long ago, from the Atures people, who were now extinct. The bird began to speak, and von Humboldt recorded the 40 words that the parrot knew, the only remaining vocabulary of what had once been an entire language.

Which Amphibian Can Survive Being Frozen

Alaska and Canada are home to several hardy frog species that somehow have to survive the icy winter. The solution found by two of them, wood frogs and chorus frogs, is that their bodies can be frozen almost solid, and they still survive. In this state of hibernation, more than two-thirds of the water in the frog's body turns to ice, and its heart stops. If you were to pick one up and cut it with a knife, it wouldn't bleed. Nonetheless, it is still alive.

bodies can be frozen almost solid and they still survive

In most animals, freezing temperatures are dangerous because ice crystals can form in their blood vessels and rupture the soft walls. Freezing can also damage skin and stop blood flow to parts of the body that are far from the heart, which can lead to frostbite. However, these amazing frogs have found a way of surviving these threats. When ice starts to form on their bodies, they begin producing extra glucose (sugar in the blood) in their livers, and this functions as antifreeze, flowing into their bodies' cells and preventing them from being damaged through freezing. Simultaneously, water drains out of the cells and into the spaces between them. This water will freeze, but it will not harm the bodies' organs. Having survived the winter, the frogs will then begin to thaw as the temperature rises in spring.

There are a number of other creatures that can survive subzero temperatures. The Siberian salamander can also survive in temperatures as low as minus 58° F (minus 50° C). It too produces a kind of chemical antifreeze before it hibernates, which protects its cells from rupturing. The Arctic woolly bear caterpillar can survive being frozen solid for 10 months in the tundra, where temperatures drop that low as well. The Arctic ground squirrel also allows its body temperature to drop below freezing—and survives. As yet, scientists haven't found an antifreeze in the squirrels like that of the wood frogs, so it's still unclear how this squirrel manages to survive the cold.

Scorpions are normally found only in warm countries, but they can withstand freezing for several weeks and can survive being underwater for two days. Their appetite is so small that some can go without any food or water for an astonishing 12 months. To top it all off, some scorpions can live for as long as 30 years.

Which Bird Can Sew ?

A number of birds have developed sewing skills to construct their nests. Examples include three birds of the warbler family: the golden-headed cisticola in Australia, the evergreen forest warbler in Africa, and the aptly named tailorbird of India.

Each of these birds has a long, thin beak, which it uses like a needle. For thread, they use spiders' silk, cotton from seeds, and fibers from the bark of trees.

To sew, the bird selects two leaves that are still growing. Holding their edges together, with a fiber in its beak, it makes a hole through both leaves and threads the fiber through. It twists both ends of this thread, locking the stitch in place. It takes about six of these stitches to turn a pair of leaves into a cup, which can then be filled with grass and used as a nest.

There are other birds that practice an even more difficult craft: weaving. In South America, orioles, oropendolas, and caciques all weave their nests. In Arica, there are a number of sparrow species that weave. They do so by tearing a fibrous strip from a leaf and threading it alternately over and under other strips. This is a difficult business, requiring some degree of forward planning and judgment since the bird has to decide how taut each strip should be, how much each wall of the planned structure should curve, and what the final shape should be. Some of the nests built in this way are extremely neat and precise.

How Do Catfish Predict Earthquakes?

There is a Japanese myth about a giant catfish, Namazu, who lives in the mud under the string of islands that make up the country of Japan. The god Kashima usually contains him, but when he drops his guard, Namuza shakes his powerful tail and causes earthquakes. The origin of the myth may have been the actual behavior of the fish.

Catfish have the most finely tuned senses of any creature. They have more taste buds than any other animals—in fact, their entire bodies are covered in them. Their senses of smell, hearing, and touch are also amazingly powerful.

A catfish can also pick up ultra-low-frequency sound using its lateral line, which is a line of small pores along the fish's side. These pores contain tiny hairlike projections that are extremely sensitive to vibrations, and people say that the fish become more active in the days leading up to an earthquake.

There is also evidence that some other animals can sense earthquakes. After the Indian Ocean tsunami in December 2004, there were numerous reports of strange animal behavior. At the Yala National Park in Sri Lanka, where 60 humans died, not one animal was killed. On India's **animals can sense earthquakes** Cuddalore coast, where thousands of people died, the local goats, buffalo, and other animals seemed to have escaped largely unharmed. There were various anecdotal reports of animals running for higher ground and abandoning their usual territories in the days leading up to the tsunami.

How could the animals have sensed that an earthquake was coming? One possible explanation is that the animals may have sensed the energy changes deep within the earth. In 1998, scientists in Japan tested this theory by observing laboratory animals' behavior while blocks of granite were crushed by machines nearby. As the pressure on the blocks grew, the animals visibly became more anxious.

Which Spider Builds Its Home Underwater ?

There is an amazing spider that is able to spend its life underwater even though, like all spiders, it cannot breathe in water. So how does it do it? The answer is that it builds itself an airtight underwater capsule, which it fills with oxygen and lives inside. It is known as the water spider, or diving bell spider.

The first stage is to weave a tight web underwater, between two plant stems. The spider manages to stay submerged by breathing the bubbles of air that get trapped in the hairs of its abdomen, and it frequently returns to the surface. Once the web is complete, the spider surfaces once more to capture a large bubble of air between its two hind legs. It swims back down with its other six legs (which is hard work since the bubble of air is buoyant) and traps the big bubble of air as well as any other smaller bubbles trapped on its abdomen under the web. It repeats this step many more times, frequently adding more threads to support and expand the web until this underwater air chamber is about the size of an acorn, making it considerably bigger than the spider itself, which is just half an inch (13 mm) long. When it needs more oxygen, the spider simply swims to the surface and brings down another bubble.

From this chamber, the spider darts out at unsuspecting prey, which may include passing tadpoles, small fish, and other pond life. Sometimes it eats insects that have been unlucky enough to fall in the water. It swims to the surface to grab them and then drags them back to its chamber.

The water spider needs to return to its bubble to eat because, like all spiders, it doesn't eat its prey whole. It inserts digestive fluids from its salivary glands into its prey, waits for the fluids to turn the insides of the prey into liquid, and then drinks that liquid. And the spider doesn't just hunt underwater. It lives in this diving bell, even mating there and bringing up its young!

Can Ants Be Farmers

The short answer is yes. Just as human farmers can have dairy farms, ants have aphid farms.

Aphids are small, soft-bodied insects that feed on the sugary sap of plants. They mainly need the nitrogen in the sap, and it takes a great deal of sap for them to get enough. This leads to lots of liquid waste, which grows out of their bodies in big sugary drops of honeydew. Honeydew may be a waste product for aphids, but ants prize it very highly.

When ants find a large group of aphids, they will milk them for their honeydew, like human farmers milking cows. The ants will tend and protect a herd of aphids in much the same way as a farmer looks after his cattle. Ants will build a shelter of leaves and soil to shield the aphids from rain or fence them in. They herd the aphids back to the ant colony at night and may then take them to a new spot to graze the next day, even selecting plants that will lead to higher production of honeydew. The ants' effort is well rewarded because the aphids can produce more than their own weight in honeydew in a single hour. Some aphid species even produce three times as much honeydew if regularly milked, just like cows.

Ants are not just aphid farmers. There are also more than 200 species of ants that grow their own food. Leaf-cutter ants do not eat the leaves they collect—instead, they grow fungus gardens on the leaves and eat the fungi. These ants tend their gardens carefully, keeping them well fertilized and free of bacteria, pests, and mold. Amazingly, the fungi that these ants grow are found nowhere else on earth.

What Animal Waste Is Used in Perfume for Humans ?

Civets are mammals found in the tropical regions of Africa and Asia. They look like a cross between a cat and a mongoose, with dark, mottled fur. Civets are tree dwellers whose diet consists of fruit, insects, worms, and some small vertebrates such as squirrels, rats, and birds.

But *civet* is also the name given to the musk produced by a gland that is found on the animal's rear end. Civets smear this oil on their homes and on rocks and branches in their territory as a sign of ownership to warn off rivals. Civet, in this sense, is a thick, oily substance with such a powerful, unpleasant smell that the tiniest whiff of it can actually make a person physically sick. Many other small mammals, including cats, badgers, skunks, and weasels, use similar secretions to mark their territory.

the **tiniest** whiff of **musk** can actually make a person physically **sick**

Because civet oil is so powerful and long-lasting, it became highly prized by perfumers. Although it smells terrible on its own, when civet oil is combined with other scents, it heightens their smell, making it stronger. It also makes them release their scent extremely slowly, so that the perfume smell lasts a long time.

You'll be happy to know that today, most perfume manufacturers use man-made oil rather than civet oil.

Coming up . . .

babies who eat their moms

2
Peculiar Parents

Which Amphibian Feeds
Her Own Skin to Her Young ?

Caecilians look like worms and live in the ground, but they are actually amphibians. They are found in the tropical regions of Asia, Africa, and South America; there are at least 170 species of them and probably many more. One of these species, *Boulengerula taitanus*, has an extraordinary way of feeding her young. When she has laid her cluster of eggs, she then curls her long body around them protectively. Once they hatch, the young start to bite her, tearing off strips of her skin. She allows this to happen until they have eaten the entire outer layer of her body. This takes place in a frenzy, which lasts about seven minutes. The family will then rest for three days, giving the mother time to grow a new layer of skin, before they dig in again.

You might think that this would hurt or damage the mother, but actually it seems to do her no harm. This is because she grows a new outer layer of skin before giving birth, making her twice as thick as before, for just this purpose. Like mammals' milk, this new skin is an excellent source of nutrients for the growing larvae. This practice is known as dermatotrophy, and the caecilian is the only amphibian known to practice it.

There is another species of caecilian that has a similarly bizarre way of feeding her young. In this species, the mother retains her eggs within her oviduct—the tube through which the egg passes—for much longer, so that the larvae hatch while still inside her. These larvae also feast on the mother's body. But rather than gnaw on her external skin, they eat the interior lining of her oviduct. In this species, the larvae can remain within their mother, cannibalizing her in this bizarre way, for up to 11 months.

Why Do Birds of Prey Encourage Their Young to Kill One Another?

As unpleasant as it may sound, many birds of prey, such as the harpy eagle and the bald eagle, will usually lay two eggs and then encourage one of the hatchlings to kill and eat the other. The parents will usually give the elder sibling most of the food and allow it to bully and harass the younger one until it dies. The favorite now eats his younger sibling, which means that the energy and nutrition that the parents invested in the second hatchling still benefit their family. The reason for this shocking approach to parenting seems to be that the birds' best chance of raising healthy offspring is to focus all their resources and energy on one chick, and so the second egg is little more than an insurance policy, in case the first egg doesn't hatch or gets destroyed in some way.

when the second egg is laid, the first is pushed out of the nest and rarely survives

The macaroni penguin does something slightly different. It also lays two eggs, but the second egg it lays is favored. The first egg is usually less than two-thirds the size of the second egg. About four days later, when the second egg is laid, the first is pushed out of the nest and rarely survives.

One reason the first egg may be so frail is that the penguins' eggs are in most danger of getting eaten or destroyed at the start of the breeding season, when the colony is just getting established. During this time, the adults are busy fighting, and birds steal many of the eggs. Another theory is that the development of the first egg is stunted because it begins while the mother is migrating from the ocean to the land. Therefore, the penguins have evolved a tendency to favor the second egg, which is more likely to result in a healthy offspring.

Which Creature Kills Its Siblings While Still in the Womb?

The sand tiger shark is a fierce-looking predator that is found in coastal waters all over the world. Despite its appearance and large size—it can grow to a length of more than 10 feet (3 m)—it is not regarded as being particularly aggressive, although there have been some reported attacks on humans.

This shark has a fascinating and gruesome way of reproducing. It has two wombs, which each contain a number of fertilized eggs. The baby sharks hatch while still inside their mother's womb, and the first ones to hatch quickly eat all the unhatched eggs. They then start to hunt down and kill one another until just two survivors remain, one in each womb.

> the **first baby** to hatch quickly **eats** all the **unhatched eggs**

Usually the first shark to hatch in each womb will be the one to survive since it had a significant head start on its siblings. One advantage of having two wombs is that the shark will usually end up producing two healthy, well-fed offspring. To provide further nourishment, the mother will continue to produce eggs for the two survivors to eat.

The offspring remain inside their mother for an astonishing two years, until they reach around 3 feet (1 m) long and are quite capable of fending for themselves. This is important because as soon as they are born, they will have to hunt and feed and defend themselves independently. Amazingly, there are reports of scientists touching the bellies of heavily pregnant sand tiger sharks and feeling the outline of the sharp, fully developed teeth of the young sharks still inside her womb!

Which Amphibian Emerges from Its Mother's Back

The Surinam toad is found in tropical South America and is a pretty weird creature, even for a toad. It is usually about 4 to 5 inches (10 to 12 cm) long, and its body is extremely flat, as if it has been stepped on. When two of these toads want to mate, they dance together in the water, somersaulting gracefully around each other. The female ejects her eggs and the male simultaneously releases his sperm so that the eggs are immediately fertilized in the water. He then spreads the toes of one foot and, using this foot like a spatula, collects the eggs and spreads them over the female's back. The pair continue to dance together, and each time they somersault, he spreads more eggs onto her back. Gradually, the skin of the female's back starts to swell up, trapping the eggs inside. Within a day or so, the skin will have regrown over the eggs, forming a strange-looking honeycomb.

The eggs now remain trapped within the female's skin, even after they hatch into tadpoles. All the while, they are absorbing nutrients from their mother and continuing to grow. Soon, you can actually see the tadpoles wriggling underneath her skin. Twenty-four days after fertilization,

you can actually see the tadpoles wriggling underneath her skin

they break through the skin of their mother's back and swim off on their own, not as tadpoles, but as fully developed miniature toads, each less than 1 inch (2.5 cm) long.

Which Insect Drinks the Blood of Its Own Young?

A type of ant recently discovered in Madagascar has an unusual and gruesome way of feeding. The Dracula ant, which is a member of the *Adetomyrma* genus, sucks the blood of its own larvae. It cuts holes into the larvae's body and feeds on the blood that oozes out. The larvae do survive being cannibalized in this way, but they are left marked and scarred.

Which Male Frog Likes to Give His Young a Leg Up in Life?

Male European midwife toads take an active and ingenious role in the reproductive process. The male will usually live near a pond, in a damp hole in the ground. When he is ready to mate, he will make a series of short, peeping calls in the hope that a female will respond. If a female does come to visit him, he holds her with his forelegs while she begins to produce eggs in strings several dozen long that rest on her thighs. The male now crouches on all fours and releases sperm onto the eggs. Then, after about 15 minutes, he lifts his legs and ties the eggs onto his thighs with the strings. Once he has collected them all, the female leaves, and he now takes care of the eggs.

The male toad carries the eggs around with him, strapped to his thighs, for a number of weeks. If the weather is dry, he will take the eggs down to the pond for a dip so that they stay moist. When it is time for the tadpoles to emerge, he goes down to the pond at night and lowers his hind legs into the

> the **male** toad
> **carries**
> the **eggs**
> **strapped**
> to his **thighs**

water. Over a couple of hours, the tadpoles will free themselves and swim off, leaving their devoted father behind.

Why Do Penduline Tits Hide Their Eggs?

Penduline tits are small, pretty birds that can reach around 4.5 inches (11 cm) in length and are found in most parts of eastern and southern Europe. The male weaves an impressive, baglike nest, which hangs from a tree, usually over the water. It is this pendulous nest that gives the birds their name. Once the nest is completed, the male calls to nearby females, hoping to persuade them to mate. The females will tour the various local nests, assessing their size and quality. In general, the female will select the biggest nest available. She indicates her choice by landing on the nest, carrying a beakful of wool, which will form the lining.

Once she has moved in, the female takes over the construction work herself. She brings in more lining and digs an entrance tube pointing downward. Once she's happy with her new home, she mates with the male and begins to lay her eggs. This is when things start to get really interesting.

Both the male and female want to leave the nest as soon as the eggs have been laid so that they can go start a second family. But they will leave only if they know that the eggs in this first nest will be looked after—both of them have already invested too much in this brood to just let the eggs die. Therefore, each tries to leave the incubation and raising of the offspring to the other.

> both the **male** and **female** want to leave the nest as soon as the **eggs** have been laid

They do this using some sneaky tactics. Usually, a clutch consists of six eggs. As a result, once a male notices that his partner has laid six eggs, he will leave at the first opportunity. That way, she will be forced to stay and look after the eggs while he can build another nest and raise another family.

To counter this risk, the female may start to hide her eggs. After laying two of them, she may bring in more nest lining and cover them up. The male doesn't seem to be able to remember how many eggs have been laid, so as long as they are out of sight, he is unaware of them. He will continue to mate with her while she continues to lay—and hide—the eggs. Eventually, she will have her six eggs, at which point she removes the lining exposing the eggs and takes off. When the unwitting male returns to the nest, he has no choice but to raise his brood single-handed while the female goes off and finds another partner.

How Do Birds Decide
Which of Their Young to Feed

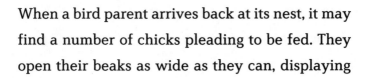

When a bird parent arrives back at its nest, it may find a number of chicks pleading to be fed. They open their beaks as wide as they can, displaying their bright red gapes (the inside of their mouths), while the parent has to decide which hungry mouth gets the food. But how does it decide?

It seems that the color of the chick's gape is crucial. Birds are more likely to feed the chicks that have the brightest, reddest gape. There are a number of possible explanations for this. In some birds, such as young linnets, the red color of the gapes comes from the blood vessels in the throat. If, however, the chick has already been fed, some of its blood will be diverted to its stomach to digest the food, leaving the gape a duller red. Therefore, a brighter gape indicates which chick has not yet been fed.

Another theory is that the parent will feed the bird with the brightest gape because this is a good indication of the bird's health. A red gape indicates that the bird has a strong immune system. According to this argument, the parent's choice serves to favor the strongest chicks, which have the best chance of living.

Some birds have evolved to take advantage of this tendency. Cuckoos lay their eggs in the nests of other birds, including dunnocks, meadow pipits, and Eurasian reed warblers. When the cuckoo chicks hatch, these interlopers will try to push the host's own chicks out of the nest and beg for food from the parent bird, seemingly using their exceptionally bright red gapes to win favor.

One type of cuckoo, the Hodgson's hawk-cuckoo, has even evolved gape-colored patches under its wings. The parent birds of the nests it invades place food into one of these patches, as if they are fooled into thinking it's the mouth of one of their young.

Why Does One Type of Lizard Lay Its Eggs Inside a Termite Nest

Reptiles lay delicate, fragile eggs that are very sensitive to temperature and moisture. In too dry an environment, the egg's shell would allow too much moisture to escape, drying out the contents and killing the embryo. If the temperature is too hot or cold, the embryo will also die. Consequently, finding the ideal spot to lay the egg is a crucial part of the reptile's reproductive process.

A number of species of monitor lizard have found a clever place to lay their eggs: in the center of a termite nest. Termite nests are one of the natural world's most astounding constructions. They are built in such a way that the temperature and humidity inside the nest remain perfectly constant. There are shafts and chimneys to create updrafts within the nest, spreading the hot air generated by the termites working in the basements of the nest. The termites manage the humidity carefully, too, bringing water up if the atmosphere inside the nest becomes too dry or hot.

This well-maintained environment is the perfect place for the monitor lizard to lay her eggs. She will rip a hole in the nest with her powerful claws and deposit her eggs in the very center of the nest. Then she simply leaves. The termites immediately begin rebuilding the nest because a change in temperature can be disastrous for their own young. Within hours, the broken walls will have been repaired and the nest's temperature and humidity restored to proper levels. The termites seem oblivious to the lizard's eggs sitting in the heart of their nest.

After a few months, the eggs hatch and the young monitor lizards struggle free of their shells. However, they are too big to climb out of the termites' tunnels, so they either have to dig their way out or wait for their mother to come and break the nest open again.

Which Animals Make the Best Parents?

We have now heard many stories of cruel and lazy animal parenthood, but what about the heroes of animal parenthood? Which parent offers the most caring, nurturing environment for its young? Is it the male emperor penguin, which spends the winter in the frozen Antarctic, huddled with his brothers, each balancing a single, precious egg on the top of his feet? Or is it perhaps the female Australian social spider, which makes the ultimate sacrifice, allowing her young to feast on her body, killing her in the process?

one **spider** allows her young to **feast on her body**, killing her in the process

Well, perhaps one way of measuring a parent's performance is to see how long the family unit stays together. If the young remain by their parents' side for a long time, it's a fair bet that they're being well looked after. According to this criterion, the clear winner is the killer whale, which is also called an orca. Killer whales form the most stable family groups of all mammals. Astonishingly, after 25 years of intensive research, watching killer whales in the coastal waters of the northeastern Pacific Ocean, researchers have not observed one single incidence of a killer whale ever leaving its mother. As far as we know, every killer whale stays with its family group for its entire life.

How Do Stick Insects Get Ants to Incubate Their Eggs

Stick insects like to keep things simple. Often, female stick insects don't even bother involving the male in the business of reproduction. Instead, a female will simply produce eggs all by herself. Then, rather than care for the eggs, the stick insect mother simply lets them drop to the ground. Yet the species endures, thanks to a number of cunningly designed evolutionary traits.

> rather than **care for** the eggs, the stick insect **mother** simply lets them **drop** to the ground

In Australia, one species of stick insect, called the spiny leaf insect, feeds almost exclusively on small, fleshy casuarina seeds, which are rich in oil and nutrients. Harvester ants like the seeds too and collect them. They store them in their nests and leave them to sprout. The female spiny leaf insect takes advantage of this by producing eggs that are small, round, and finely ridged, exactly like casuarina seeds. The harvester ants can't tell the difference, so they collect the insect's eggs along with the seeds and store them all together. Later, when the ants come to eat their stores, they find that only some of the seeds have sprouted tasty attachments. They eat only those and leave the eggs alone.

Eventually, the eggs hatch, and we might imagine that this would put the infant stick insects in considerable danger. They are, after all, uninvited intruders in the ants' nest. However, the stick insects' gift for mimicry protects the infants once again. When they hatch, they look and move exactly like newborn ants and simply walk out of the nest and climb up the casuarina tree to start the process again.

3
Crafty Critters

Which Creature
Can Drop Its Tail Off ?

Many types of lizard, including skinks, have the ability to drop off their tails when threatened by a predator. The tails have special fracture points, so that if these lizards are being chased or grabbed by a predator, the tail will drop off. Amazingly, the tail will continue to wriggle, confusing the predator and creating the illusion of a continued struggle. With luck, this buys the lizard enough time to escape.

In the weeks after losing a tail, the lizard will usually be able to grow another, although this one will contain cartilage rather than bone and will often be smaller than the original tail. Sometimes, if the first tail doesn't drop off fully, the new tail will grow alongside it, giving the lizard the freaky appearance of having two tails.

Glass lizards do something even more surprising. Like skinks, they drop their tails when threatened.

But when a glass lizard's tail drops off, it breaks into a number of pieces—shattering like glass. A glass lizard's tail makes up as much as two-thirds of the creature's length, so it is a shocking and extraordinary sight when it shatters—it looks as if the creature has spontaneously smashed into pieces (and technically it has). Often the broken pieces of the tail will continue to twitch while the glass lizard itself remains motionless, confusing and distracting the predator and helping the lizard make its escape.

> when a **glass lizard's** tail drops off, it **shatters** like **glass**

Why Do Moles Squeeze Earthworms

Moles are cute, furry, burrowing mammals that are around 6 inches (15 cm) long and weigh 3.5 ounces (100 g). They spend most of their lives foraging in a network of underground tunnels, through which they burrow at incredible speed.

Moles have short, powerful legs and very broad front feet, which they use for digging. Just one small mole can dig its way through an amazing 46 feet (14 m) of soil in only one hour.

Moles have an active, high-energy lifestyle, which means they usually need to eat their own weight in food each day. Their diet can include insects, spiders, grubs, and even an occasional mouse, but their main food is earthworms. When it finds an earthworm, a mole will pull it through its paws, squeezing it tightly to force out any earth and mud from the worm's guts.

Then the mole will either eat the worm or keep it for later. Moles have a toxin in their saliva that can paralyze earthworms, so they often bite off the worm's head, paralyzing but not killing it. They store the headless worm in a specially constructed underground room. Scientists have found well-stocked mole pantries containing as many as a thousand paralyzed earthworms.

How Do Fireflies Tell Fire-lies**?**

Fireflies are celebrated for their wonderful ability to produce cold light (meaning that there is no heat emitted) through a process called bioluminescence, in which the light is produced by the reaction of two chemicals in the presence of oxygen. Female fireflies use these green, yellow, and pale red lights to attract a mate. They flash their lights in a distinct pattern that is unique to their species and acts as a signal to nearby males. This system helps the males and females of each species to find eligible partners and to avoid wasting time paying visits to fireflies of other species.

However, some crafty female fireflies have found a way around this system. *Photuris* fireflies, which are also known as "femme fatale fireflies," can copy the flash patterns of other species in order to attract these males. When the male flies down, he is

female fireflies use light to attract a mate

expecting to find a friendly and receptive female of his own species. Instead, he finds a hungry femme fatale, which quickly kills him and eats him for dinner.

Which Spider Looks Like a Blob of Bird Poop

There is a spider, appropriately known as the bird-dropping spider, that looks just like a lump of bird poop. It has a gray-and-white body, and it is usually found with its legs tucked in, curled up in a ball, sitting on a leaf, just where a blob of bird muck might land. It may not be pretty, but this disguise is far from unique—a number of caterpillars use a similar camouflage.

Why would any creature choose to look like bird poop? Well, first, it protects them from predators. This spider's most likely attackers are birds, which naturally avoid eating the poop of other birds. Second,

Why would any creature choose to look like bird poop?

it helps them hunt food of their own. The spider's prey are unlikely to see any threat in the common sight of bird droppings and so may come far closer than is good for them.

Which Spider Hunts Like a Gaucho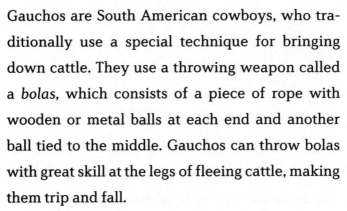

Gauchos are South American cowboys, who traditionally use a special technique for bringing down cattle. They use a throwing weapon called a *bolas*, which consists of a piece of rope with wooden or metal balls at each end and another ball tied to the middle. Gauchos can throw bolas with great skill at the legs of fleeing cattle, making them trip and fall.

In many parts of the world, including South America, the bolas spider uses a similar technique to snare its prey. It is about the size of a pea and colored black and white. When darkness starts to fall, the spider goes hunting. First it lays a line of nonsticky silk on the underside of a twig or leaf. Then it hangs from this line, using two of its legs.

Next it spins a line of sticky silk, about 1 inch (2.5 cm) long, with a sticky blob of silk at the end, like the weighted end of the bolas. Now the spider simply hangs there, dangling its line, which glints in the twilight.

In these first few hours of the night, the spider is hunting for cutworm moths. Eventually, one will appear. The moth may be attracted by the light glinting off the sticky silk. It is also attracted by the scent that the spider emits, which matches the perfume used in cutworm moth courtship. As the moth gets closer, the spider swishes the bolas, swiping the moth into its mouth. If the spider hasn't caught anything in about 15 minutes, it will reel in its line and eat it (perhaps because the line will have lost its stickiness).

Later, when these moths are no longer active, the spider rests until about midnight. Then it goes hunting again, but this time it has a new target: a moth called the smoky tetanolita. The spider now begins to produce a different scent, this one designed to attract its new prey, like a skillful fisherman varying his bait to catch a different type of fish.

Which Spider Builds a Life-Size Model of Itself

Many types of spiders decorate their webs, and these decorations seem to serve a number of functions. Some spiders use silk ornaments to strengthen the web. Other decorations seem designed to make the web more visible, either to deter large animals from accidentally walking into it and destroying it or to attract prey. Scientists in Taiwan have recently observed one type of spider building a life-size replica of itself as a decoy to fool predators. No other creature is known to build a model of itself in this way.

A number of species of orb spider are known to decorate their webs with curious materials, including discarded egg sacs, plants, and the remains of prey. Until recently, this kind of decoration was believed to be used as camouflage. But scientists observing the spiders found that wasps were actually more likely to attack decorated webs than plain ones, suggesting that the decorations weren't very successful camouflage.

Observing another species of orb spider, *Cyclosa mulmeinensis,* on Orchid Island, off the southeast coast of Taiwan, the scientists noticed that it built pellets using egg sacs and dead insect bodies that were exactly the same size and shape as its own body. These pellets would appear to wasps to be the same color as the spider and to reflect light in the same way. When wasps attacked the web, more often than not they would attack the decoy rather than the spider, suggesting that while these decoys might attract more wasps than an undecorated web, they nonetheless made the spider safer overall.

Do Fish Fish for Fish

There's a type of fish that has a very crafty technique for catching its prey. It is called an

the bait is its own **tongue**, which is long and thin and wriggles like a **worm**

anglerfish because it uses bait just like a fisherman. However, the bait it uses is its own tongue, which is long and thin and wriggles like a worm. The anglerfish sits on a reef with its mouth wide open and its tongue wriggling, looking just like a juicy, tasty worm. When a curious fish comes closer, thinking it found a snack, the anglerfish sucks it into its mouth and enjoys a snack itself.

The anglerfish is the only fish that is known to use this technique, but there is a kind of turtle that does something very similar. The alligator snapping turtle is a big, ferocious predator that can weigh as much as 220 pounds (100 kg). Its jaws are hooked and have a sharp cutting edge made of horn. It is so fierce that if you approach it on land, it may well attack you.

The alligator snapping turtle lies at the bottom of a lake with its mouth open, using its tongue to tempt passing fish. Like the anglerfish, the snapping turtle has a long, thin, bright red tongue, which wriggles in such a way as to perfectly mimic a worm. The turtle's technique is slightly different from that of the anglerfish. Instead of sucking its prey into its mouth, it snaps its powerful jaws shut, often chopping the fish in half.

How Do Japanese Crows Crack Open Walnuts?

Carrion crows are found throughout the forests of Japan, as are walnut trees. Until recently, carrion crows had never been able to crack open those tasty and nutritious treats because their beaks were not strong enough. Many birds do manage to crack open similarly difficult foods by dropping them from the air—for example, bearded vultures live mainly on a diet of bone marrow, which they get by dropping bones from a great height, cracking them open. The similarly ingenious Egyptian vulture likes to eat ostrich eggs, which are full of nutrients, but their shells are very thick and difficult to crack open. So the vultures drop rocks onto the eggs, breaking the shells. Walnuts can be cracked open by being dropped, but they have to be dropped as many as 50 times, so it's a lot of work for a small snack.

In 1990, the ingenious carrion crows of Sendai City came up with an impressive solution. They started using cars. The birds wait at the city's traffic lights, holding walnuts in their beaks. When the lights turn red, they swoop down and place the nut in front of a car's tires. When the lights turn green, the cars drive over the nuts, cracking them open. The birds wait for the lights to turn red again, then hop back down into the road and pick up their dinner. This behavior is slowly spreading as other crows observe it happening and then take it up themselves. One of the most fascinating aspects of this behavior is that the crows seem to have learned to use traffic lights and to understand something of how they work, because other stretches of road would be too dangerous.

Why Do Birds Pretend to Be Injured?

Rather than build elaborate nests in trees, a number of birds, such as lapwings and plovers, simply lay their eggs on open ground—on marshes, grasslands, or beaches. This is a simpler solution than building an intricate nest, but it means the eggs are more vulnerable to predators such as foxes. One way to protect the eggs is to camouflage them, and so birds that nest in this way tend to produce eggs with mottled patterns to make them invisible against the gravelly ground. When the chicks hatch, the parent birds carry away the broken bits of shell so that their shiny white interiors don't attract predators.

This camouflage doesn't always work. If a predator gets close to the chicks, it's likely to recognize them as a meal, so the mother will try a different trick: she will pretend to be injured. When predators approach, lapwings and plovers hop away from their nests, dragging a wing along the ground as if they are hurt. To ensure that they attract the predator's attention, they may start screaming as if in pain or distress.

A predator such as a stoat is likely to be far more tempted by the prospect of a fully grown adult bird than a handful of eggs or chicks, and so it follows, getting gradually dragged away from the young birds. As the predator gets closer to the mother, at the last minute she suddenly flies away, as if she has been miraculously healed. However, the stoat has by now been led so far away from the nest that, even if it had spotted the eggs in the first place, it now has no way of retracing its steps and finding the eggs again.

Other birds seem to have developed this trick to an even more advanced degree. Instead of faking an injury, purple sandpipers on an Arctic tundra run away from their nests with both wings trailing behind, raising their feathers while making a squeaking sound that bears no resemblance to their usual calls. Thus, they look and sound just like a scuttling mouse or lemming, both of which are particularly tempting prey for arctic foxes, the most likely audience for the performance. In the United States, the green-tailed towhee also tries to mimic another kind of appealing prey. If a coyote approaches, it will run from its nest while lifting its tail. This at first glance makes it look a bit like a chipmunk, which is the main prey of local coyotes.

Do Animals Tell Lies ?

A number of bird species are known to deceive one another for their own gain, taking advantage of the communal warning system by which many birds depend on one another for their safety.

Often a forest will contain many species of birds of a similar size, which are all threatened by the arrival of a larger predator such as a hawk. Consequently, birds have developed a wonderfully resourceful warning system, in which the first bird to spot the danger will sound the alarm by giving a particular type of call, which is usually written as *seet*. It is a soft, short, high-pitched call, which is clear and easily understood but difficult to locate, thus minimizing the danger for the caller. (Obvious-ly, an alarm call that significantly endangered the signaler would be of very limited value.) On hear-ing the *seet* call, all the birds in the area will drop what they are doing, find shelter, and remain quiet.

But this system also presents opportunities for deception. In the Amazonian rain forest, com-munities of small birds operate a warning system while they rummage through the leaf litter look-ing for tasty insects. Here two species of bird of-ten keep watch: antshrikes, which perch under the shade of the canopy, and shrike tanagers, which act as lookouts above the canopy. Doing this job means that these birds have less time to forage for insects, so the other birds reward them by let-ting them have some of the insects that they find. Sometimes, though, the lookouts will lie. If they spot a particular tasty-looking insect being dug up, they may give a warning call even though there is no actual danger. The other birds will flee for safety, and the caller will come and grab the insect.

Various monkey species use a similar system

of alarm calls. Vervet monkeys have at least five different calls, which give detailed warnings as to which direction the danger is coming from, whether it is from the ground or the air, and how urgent and threatening the danger is. Again, however, sometimes the lookouts tell lies. In one example, researchers witnessed one monkey watching another monkey digging up a large root. Just as it was about to pull this tempting prize from the ground, the first monkey shouted the alarm for *snake,* which sent the other monkey scuttling up into the trees for safety. Then the crafty lookout came down and grabbed the tasty root, with no snake in sight. In a more detailed study, capuchin monkeys were found to do the same thing. In an Argentinean national park, scientists found that the monkeys sounded the alarm more frequently when pieces of banana were placed in the open.

Of course, the two main preoccupations of most creatures are food and reproduction, so as we might expect, there are also examples of animals that tell lies for the purposes of attracting a mate.

For instance, male domestic chickens are known to produce a specific type of call when they have found food. Sometimes these chickens give this call when in fact they have no food, purely to lure the female to come closer.

Which Bird Is an Expert Impressionist?

In the forests of southern Australia lives a bird with an extraordinary talent. It is the male Australian lyrebird, and it sings one of the most beautiful and complex songs of any bird. When it's time to mate, the female lyrebirds make a tour of the males' display mounds in the forest to inspect their potential partners. The males are extraordinary-looking, with cream-colored, fanlike tail feathers. When the males display, they bend these tail feathers forward, completely covering themselves.

At the same time, they sing a variety of songs, which are not only pleasing to the ear but also full of clever mimicry. The male lyrebird's courtship song incorporates many amazing trills and warbles and also mimics the songs of almost every other bird in the neighboring area. Ornithologists are said to be able to recognize the calls of more than a dozen different birds in the lyrebird's playlist. Presumably, this talent has evolved in response to the female's attraction to ever more complex and varied performances.

Perhaps the most impressive aspect of the lyrebird's act is that these songs are not just inherited traits, passed down through the generations. Rather, each individual bird has a talent for spontaneous mimicry and can quickly learn and incorporate new sounds. This is demonstrated by the great speed with which these birds add the sounds of human activity into their songs when their territories are close to human settlements. Lyrebirds observed near populated areas have been known to mimic the

lyrebirds mimic the sounds of **chain saws,** car alarms, **barking dogs,** camera motors, **car horns,** welding machines, and crying babies

sounds of chain saws, car alarms, barking dogs, camera motors, car horns, welding machines, and crying babies in their recitals. Some are also said to have learned tunes that they've overheard being played by musicians.

Why Do Owls Collect Poop

A large proportion of a burrowing owl's diet consist of dung beetles, and so these wise birds have come up with an ingenious way to attract their prey. Dung beetles, of course, love nothing more than poop; in fact, their whole society is based on it. Taking advantage of this, burrowing owls collect the droppings of cows, horses, and other large mammals and carry them back to their burrows, lining their nests with the smelly stuff. This bait attracts the dung beetles, which scuttle their way to the burrow's entrance, hoping for a tasty meal. Instead, they soon find that the hungry owl waiting there deserves its reputation for intelligence.

Which Bird Turns Itself into an Umbrella ?

Green-backed herons are perhaps the craftiest fishermen of all the birds. They use a number of sophisticated techniques to catch their prey and are also able to quickly learn new tricks. One of the heron's clever techniques is to turn itself into an umbrella. On a hot day, a wading heron may spread its broad wings, creating a patch of cool, shady water in the lake or river where it is hunting. Remaining quite still, the heron then waits for a fish to swim into this pleasant patch of shade before grabbing it in its beak.

This is merely one of this particular heron's impressive fishing techniques. In Japan, green-backed herons seem to have recently learned to fish with bait, having presumably picked up the habit from observing humans. In a public park, where people come to feed the exotic fish, herons have started picking up morsels of bread and dropping them onto the surface of the lake, as if feeding the fish. When a hungry fish comes to the surface to take the bread, the heron grabs it in its beak. Herons have also been seen using insects as bait in the same way.

The heron also uses another even more sophisticated tactic. As fishermen will tell you, fish are naturally curious. It is not always necessary to offer food to get them to rise to the surface; something shiny or colorful will do the trick just as well. A bird called the little egret has black legs with bright yellow feet. To attract fish, the little egret shakes one of its brightly colored feet on the surface of the water, tempting fish to come to investigate. The green-backed heron has learned to do something similar, dangling small feathers on the water's surface, and this also seems to work.

Which Birds Can Chat with Badgers

The honeyguide is a small, dull-looking bird, distantly related to woodpeckers. It is found in Asia and Africa. The honeyguide likes to eat beeswax and bee larvae as well as other insects. In fact, it is the only animal of any kind that is known to be able to digest wax.

In Asia, bees tend to nest in relatively open, unprotected sites, hanging from the ceiling of a cave, for example. Honeyguides have no trouble raiding these nests.

But African bees tend to build their nests in tight places, such as holes in trees or small spaces between rocks. Honeyguides can find these nests, but they can't get in, so they recruit the help of a creature called a honey badger, also known as a ratel. Ratels love honey, and they have the necessary claws and physical strength to break into all kinds of nests. Amazingly, these two very different species have learned to work together.

When the honeyguide finds a ratel, it perches nearby and calls to it, giving a distinctive, chattering cry. The honey badger responds with a series of guttural growls and begins to follow the bird. The honeyguide flies off, frequently stopping, calling, and fluttering its tail at the ratel to make sure it's still following, while the ratel answers these calls by growling back. When the bird reaches the hive, it perches above the hive and gives a different call. The ratel apparently understands what this means—that the nest is nearby—and begins digging for it. Once the ratel finds the nest, the bees attack it, swarming around its head and stinging it. The ratel responds by farting into the nest hole, and the smell it produces must be as unbearable to the bees as it is to humans since most of the bees now flee. Using its claws, the ratel tears out the honeycombs and carries them away. The honeyguide now swoops down to forage in what's left of the wreckage of the nest, feasting on the dead bees, grubs, and honeycomb.

> the **ratel** responds by **farting** into the nest hole

Honey badgers are not the only animals that honeyguides have learned to work with. They also collaborate with humans, specifically the Boran people of East Africa. When they want to find honey, the Boran bushmen give a specific whistle, known as a *fuulido*, to summon the honeyguide. The bird will then lead them to a secluded bees' nest, just as it would lead a ratel. According to tradition, once the bushmen are finished, they leave a gift behind for the honeyguide to thank it for its help.

Which Animal Is Nature's Most Unlikely Impressionist?

One candidate must be the tiny blister beetle larva, which manages to impersonate a creature hundreds of times its size. Or, rather, it manages to do so with the help of hundreds of its siblings. A bunch of blister beetle larvae group together into the beelike shape of a female digger bee to fool a male bee into trying to mate with them.

Why, you ask? To hitch a ride.

When the group attracts a male digger bee, rather than get crushed, the larvae climb onto the bee and cling to its body with their tiny claws. The bee, most likely confused, flies off to find another mate. When he finds one, the beetle larvae jump onto her. This is the last leg of their trip.

The fertilized female now returns to her nest, where she has filled a number of open cells with pollen. Here the beetle larvae dismount to enjoy their new home, where they will grow in safety, feasting on the bees' eggs and honey, before emerging as adult blister beetles.

Are Sheep Smarter Than We Think?

Sheep don't possess the most thrilling intellects of the animal kingdom, but they perhaps deserve more credit than they are given. For one thing, they have excellent memories. They can remember the faces of sheep and people for up to two years. They can also be trained to remember the rocks and streams that mark the boundaries of their territory and then pass on this information to their young. This is obviously an extremely useful trait from a shepherd's point of view. Some flocks of sheep will retain this information for centuries, passing it on from one generation to the next.

Sheep have also displayed some even more daring talents. Recently, for example, sheep in Yorkshire, England, have taught themselves how to roll across cattle grids to raid the local villagers' gardens. Daredevil sheep have been observed getting a running start and then rolling across the hoof-proof grids in a ball like army commandos. Since these grids are about 8 feet (2.5 m) wide, this is no mean feat. The hungry sheep are also said to have learned to climb or hurdle over fences up to 5 feet (1.5 m) high. So you see, not all sheep are sheepish!

> **daredevil sheep have been observed rolling across hoof-proof grids in a ball like army commandos**

How Do Stoats Hypnotize Rabbits?

There is a type of weasel called the stoat that is one of the animal kingdom's most extraordinary predators. They eat a varied diet, including birds, eggs, insects, and small mammals. They also hunt rabbits, even though rabbits are much bigger than stoats and can weigh 10 times as much. Rabbits are also strong, alert, agile, and very fast, which makes them an extremely difficult meal to catch. However, stoats have learned how to get around all of these challenges—by using hypnosis.

The stoat stealthily approaches the rabbit, creeping toward it through the long grass. When it gets within range, it deliberately draws attention to itself, dancing, jumping, and chasing its tail. It's a bizarre performance. The stoat somersaults, then backflips. It vanishes into the grass, then leaps up in the air again. The rabbit is mesmerized as the dancing stoat gradually gets closer and closer. Suddenly, the stoat leaps toward the rabbit and bites into the back of its neck, smashing the back of its skull with its teeth. The rabbit may twitch once or twice before collapsing, dead. The businesslike stoat now drags the heavy corpse back to its burrow.

Which Bird Builds a Decoy Nest?

In the Australian bush, a type of bird called the yellow-rumped thornbill is terrorized by curra-wongs, which are big, aggressive birds that attack the thornbills' nests and steal their eggs. Their so-lution is to build a second, decoy nest on top of the active one. The decoy nest is simple a cup-shaped depression, while underneath it sits the real nest, with a hidden entrance. Currawongs attack from above, so if they see the empty decoy nest, they are likely to leave it alone and move on without investigating further, unaware of the active nest underneath. Thanks to this clever construction, thornbill nests suffer far less from currawong raids than their neighbors' do.

How Do Squirrels Deceive Rattlesnakes?

A squirrel's tail is one of the most useful tools of any mammal's. First, squirrels use their tails to balance when walking along a precarious branch. If they do fall, their tail acts as a parachute, catching the air and slowing the squirrel's descent. When running on the ground, squirrels use their tails as a fifth limb and rudder to help them change direction at speed. If a bird attacks, a squirrel can shelter under its big bushy tail, making it impossible for the bird to grab it in its talons. In the summer, a tail makes an effective sunshade, while in the winter, it's like a wonderfully soft, warm quilt, which helps the squirrel to conserve precious heat and energy.

Another exciting use for the squirrel's tail has recently been discovered. Snakes are one of the squirrel's most dangerous predators, but squirrels have found a way to use their tails to protect themselves against one group, namely the rattlesnake. Rattlesnakes have a poor sense of sight, but they have another way of "seeing" their prey, using their extremely sensitive heat-sensing organs. These organs consist of two small pits, one on either side of the snake's head, between its eyes and its nostrils. These pits help snakes detect the size, shape, distance, and direction of prey purely from sensing its heat energy.

When a squirrel is confronted by a rattlesnake, it fills its tail with blood, raising the tail's temperature. Since the rattlesnake can only really see things if they are warm, this makes the squirrel look twice as big as it otherwise would, which can be enough to make the rattlesnake warily slink off, leaving the squirrel in peace. The most amazing part of this ingenious technique is that squirrels don't bother to heat up their tails for other snakes. They do it solely for snakes that have these heat-sensing organs.

What Is Particularly Devious About the Alcon Blue Butterfly

The Alcon blue butterfly (*Maculinea alcon*) is an extremely attractive specimen that is found in Europe and northern Asia, where it brightens up many summer afternoons. However, as delicate and charming as they look, Alcon blues are among nature's most devious schemers when it comes to raising their young.

The process begins when the butterfly lays its eggs on the leaves of a gentian plant. When the caterpillars hatch from the eggs, they burrow into the flower's buds and feed. They grow much larger and eventually drop to the ground. Here the caterpillar is found by ants. At this point, the caterpillar begins to produce a chemical pheromone, which somehow seems to induce the worker ants to treat it like one of their own precious larvae. The ants take the caterpillar back to their nest and begin to feed it.

Yet the caterpillar is not satisfied with food and safe lodgings. Now its chemical signals instruct the ants to give it preferential treatment. If the nest is disturbed, the ants will rush the caterpillar to safety while ignoring their own young. For an astonishing two years, the ants will continue to feed the interloper until it is fully grown and ready to take its adult form. When it emerges from its pupal stage, the butterfly is at last recognized for the imposter that it is.

This story of deception and intrigue has one more amazing twist. The butterfly does not always make it to its adult stage because another crafty creature may further complicate things. While the alcon blue is still a caterpillar, a female ichneumon wasp may appear. This parasitic wasp seems to be able to sense when an ants' nest is hosting an alcon blue. When the wasp enters the nest, the ants panic and try to attack her. In response, the wasp emits a powerful pheromone of her own, which not only repels the ants from her but also makes them attack one another. In the confusion, she lands on the caterpillar and injects an egg deep inside its body.

After the wasp flies off, the ants continue life as normal. They feed the caterpillar as attentively as always, and it eventually turns into a chrysalis. But when the chrysalis opens, it's not an alcon blue butterfly that emerges but an ichneumon wasp, which has devoured the butterfly pupa from the inside out!

Coming up...

4
Mind-Boggling Biology

What Happened to
the Exploding Toads of Hamburg ?

In April 2005, strange reports started to come out of Hamburg, Germany. According to local people, toads around a pond had begun to explode spontaneously, as many as a thousand in a matter of days. According to reports, the toads were seen crawling on the ground as their bodies gradually swelled to the bursting point. Then they would explode, propelling their entrails up to 3 feet (1 m) into the air. Local people began to worry, and the authorities warned that children and dogs should be kept away from the area. The pond itself was sealed off and became known as the "pond of death."

So what was causing this bizarre phenomenon? Were local people imagining it? Was it some kind of elaborate hoax? Or was there a more logical explanation? Scientists speculated that the cause could be some unknown virus or fungus in the pond; there had been cases of foreign horses at a nearby racetrack becoming infected by a type of fungus. Other suggested explanations included the over-use of pesticides and increased ultraviolet radiation caused by the thinning of the ozone layer.

One of Germany's top experts on amphibians, Franz Mutschmann, decided to investigate. He began collecting the toads' carcasses and performing autopsies on them. He noticed that all of the toads were missing their livers and that each had a precise circular incision on its back, small enough to be the work of a bird's beak. He concluded that crows were attacking the toads and tearing out their livers. In response, the toads would fill themselves with air as a defense mechanism. But instead of deflating like they usually do, the toads' blood vessels and lungs ruptured, sending their intestines flying into the air.

But why were the crows taking just the toads' livers rather than eating the whole creature? Crows know that toads' skin is poisonous, so they worked out how to get a snack without eating the skin.

Why Are Poison-Dart Frogs Endangered?

The amazing poison-dart frogs of Central and South America produce some of the most toxic poisons of any animals. The frogs are so toxic that they have few predators. They have developed extremely bright, vividly colored skins to attract mates and to alert any potential predator to the danger they pose.

The most lethal of them all is perhaps the golden poison frog, which is believed to be the world's most poisonous vertebrate. The frog is just 2 inches (5 cm) long, but it contains enough poison to kill between 10 and 20 adult humans. The tiniest drop of this poison will disable a person's nervous system, causing the muscles to contract uncontrollably, leading to heart failure. Chickens and dogs have been killed simply by coming into contact with a paper towel that one of these frogs had walked across.

One might imagine that a creature with such emphatic defensive attributes would face few dangers, and yet many species of poison-dart frog are actually endangered. Ironically, the frogs' very toxicity may be the reason. The indigenous people of the Amazon rain forest have learned to harvest the frogs' poison by catching them, roasting them on a spit, and collecting the poison as it drips from their skin. The resulting sticky paste is then used to tip their arrows for hunting trips or warfare.

Which Beetle Seeks Out Fire ?

What would you do if a raging forest fire was heading straight toward you? You'd probably want to get away as quickly as possible. However, one bizarre little beetle does the opposite. The black jewel beetle, also known as the firebug, can sense the faintest whiff of a forest fire at great distances. And when it gets the scent, it heads straight for the inferno.

when the **black jewel** **beetle** gets the scent of a fire, it heads straight for **the inferno**

The reason is that the black jewel beetle likes to make its home in the charred trees, ideally as soon as possible after a fire. Most creatures either flee a fire or die, which means that a charred tree is likely to be free of any predators. This means that a hot, charred tree provides a haven where the black jewel beetle can mate recklessly and lay its eggs safely without fear of predators or competition.

The way the jewel beetle senses a distant fire is fascinating and not yet fully understood. The beetle has a tiny infrared sensor under one of its legs, which allows it to detect the faintest whiff of wood smoke from as far as 50 miles (80 km) away. Scientists are hoping to harness this amazing technology to develop an early-warning system for forest fires.

Why Do Elephants Die of Hunger

Elephants graze on the open plains of Africa and Asia, eating a fibrous diet of grass and leaves. This wears down their teeth very quickly. Other animals with a similar diet face the same problem, which they deal with in a variety of ways. Rabbits, for example, have teeth with open roots that continue growing throughout their lives to replace the constant wear at the other end.

Elephants' teeth grow in a different way. Most mammals' teeth emerge vertically from the jaw, but elephants' teeth come in from back to front. As the old teeth are worn away, the elephants' new molars emerge at the back of the jaw and gradually push through to the front until the old ones drop out. There is a limit to how many sets of teeth an elephant can produce. After its last pair is worn out, the animal is unable to produce any more teeth, and even if it is healthy and capable in all other respects, with no way of chewing its food, it starves to death.

Elephants are not alone in this: kangaroos too have a limited number of sets of teeth. Kangaroos can produce only four pairs of molars. Once these are worn away, any kangaroo that has managed to survive all the other dangers facing an aging large mammal will nonetheless die of starvation.

Do Any Animals Take Medicine

A number of mammals have learned how to be their own doctors. Chimpanzees eat the bristly leaves of the *Aspilia* plant, which contains a special oil that kills the bacteria, intestinal worms, and other parasites that can infect their stomachs. The chimps pluck off the plant's leaves, mash them up in their hands, and chew them before swallowing. The leaves have little or no nutritional value, so the only reason to eat them seems to be their medicinal value. This theory is supported by the fact that the chimps seem to find the taste bitter, because when they eat the leaves, they pull faces and give other indications of an unpleasant taste.

In another example, Rwandan mountain gorillas travel to special parts of the forest where they eat fistfuls of the earth, which is rich in special minerals that their normal diet lacks.

In the Amazon rain forest, macaws peck at exposed banks of mineral clays to get essential minerals. Sheep too have been shown to seek out certain foods to make them feel better. When given a diet high in acids, which can cause digestive problems, sheep will actively choose foods that contain substances that help to soothe their system. Furthermore, tests have shown that sheep with specific digestive problems will be more likely to select just the right foods to make them feel better.

What Happens If You Turn a Shark Upside Down?

an overturned shark goes into a **comalike** state for 15 minutes

If you turn a shark onto its back, it will become completely immobile. For some reason, an overturned shark goes into a comalike state (called tonic immobility) for 15 minutes, during which it remains totally unresponsive. Its dorsal fins straighten, and its breathing and muscle contractions become more steady and re-laxed. No one knows the reason for this strange re-action, but even the scent of food is not enough to wake the shark once it is in this state.

Why Do Rhinos Charge into Trees

Rhinos have very poor eyesight, which makes it difficult for them to spot danger. Consequently, they have developed what to us might seem to be a rather silly response. When they spot anything that looks remotely like danger, they will charge at it, even if it means they end up crashing into trees or boulders. Despite their bulky size, rhinos are amazingly quick, charging at speeds of up to 28 miles (45 km) per hour, which is faster than even the top speed of the world-record-breaking Jamaican sprinter Usain Bolt.

rhinos charge at speeds of up to 28 miles per hour, faster than Usain Bolt

Why Do Ostriches Eat Stones?

Anyone witnessing an ostrich picking up and swallowing mouthfuls of grit and stones might think it isn't too smart. But this collection of gravel actually serves a crucial purpose.

One of the defining features of birds is that they have a beak rather than a mouth full of teeth. Beaks are light, powerful, and aerodynamic, but they are no good for chewing, and a bird's food is often swallowed whole. Luckily, deep inside its stomach, birds have a second chamber called the gizzard. A gizzard looks like a flat, round purse, with thick, ridged walls that contract rhythmically to grind the bird's food and break it down (with the help of digestive juices produced by the stomach's first chamber).

In fact, all birds have a gizzard, but birds that live on seeds need extra abrasive power to break down the seeds, so they fill their gizzard with grit. Grit weighs less than a mouthful of teeth, and its location in the stomach is more aerodynamic and better balanced for flight. Nonetheless, the extra weight is still a consideration, so some birds get rid of their grit at certain times of the year when their diet switches to insects. Birds that spend very little time in the air, such as turkeys, chickens, and ostriches, have large gizzards that contain a lot of grit.

Coming up...

crabs use
weapons

5
Vicious Varmints

What's the Best Way to Fight a Crocodile?

Crocodiles are one of the most enduring species on earth, and for good reason: they are ferocious predators. If you're faced with a crocodile, your best bet is to get away as quickly as possible. The fastest crocodiles can run at only about 11 miles (18 km) per hour, which is slower than most people can sprint, so on land a person should be able to run away from a crocodile. It could also help to run from side to side since crocodiles are not good at making sharp turns. But don't climb a tree to escape. Crocodiles are incredibly patient and will wait under a tree for days if they are likely to get a good meal out of it.

However, crocodiles live and hunt in the water, so that's where an attack is most likely to take place. If that happens, it's said that the best thing to do is attack its eyeballs with your fingers. Apparently, the crocodile will

crocodiles will wait under a tree for days if they are likely to get a good meal out of it

automatically open its jaws and let you go since the eyes are the most sensitive part of its body.

A 26-year-old man named Hillary Amuma tested this theory when he was attacked by a crocodile while fishing in the Tana River in Ethiopia. The crocodile grabbed his left thigh and began to drag him into the water. Amuma says at that point he remembered the traditional Pokomo tribe method his grandfather had taught him. He threw away his fishing gear and jabbed his fingers into the crocodile's eyes. The animal let Amuma go but then got him again. Once more Amuma attacked the crocodile's eyes, and this time he escaped. "The Pokomo say a crocodile fears being touched in the eyes, and once that is done, it becomes immobile and lets go," he said. "A real Pokomo man cannot be scared by a crocodile."

Which Spider Crushes Its Prey to Death?

Many spiders have elaborate and clever ways of catching their prey. Some build sticky webs for insects to walk into or throw small webs over their prey. Others jump onto their prey, or chase it, or ambush it. One species builds a trapdoor and suddenly appears as if from out of the earth. Another spider mimics ants so that it can then eat them. One even hunts underwater. But once these predators have caught their prey, they all tend to kill it in the same direct fashion: they bite it, paralyzing it with their venom, and then devour it with their sharp, powerful fangs.

Hackled orb weaver spiders have no fangs, which means they have no way of paralyzing their prey. Instead, to kill a single moth or beetle, this spider will weave more than 460 feet (140 m) of silk, performing more than 28,000 individual movements to wrap its prey tighter and tighter. This silk shroud becomes so tight that it breaks the insect's legs and forces its eyes into its head, often killing it outright. The hackled orb weaver is the only spider known to crush its prey to death in this way.

Which Fish Spits Its Prey to Death?

The archerfish has a very impressive technique for catching its prey. It is unique among fish because it can squirt precise jets of water from its mouth to shoot insects down from the waterside leaves and stems where they perch. The archerfish can spit up to 10 feet (3 m). It is extremely accurate, almost always hitting its target with the first shot. This is particularly impressive when you consider that the archerfish is underwater, which means that its view of the insect is refracted and distorted by the water's surface. Somehow the fish takes this into account when it aims.

Then, within 100 milliseconds of the insect's being knocked off its perch, the fish will start swimming to the exact spot in the water where it knows the insect will fall. Amazingly, the archerfish can predict this so accurately that it arrives to collect the insect just 50 milliseconds after it hits the water, ensuring that no other predator can sneak in and steal the fish's meal.

Which Bird Kicks Its Prey to Death?

The secretary bird has an unusual way of killing its prey—it stamps its victims to death. It is an extremely tall, gangly bird that can reach 4 feet (1.2 m) in height. It can fly if necessary, but it has largely lost the habit, probably because it is so successful at hunting on the ground. It stalks across the grassland of Africa, often walking as much as 15 miles (24 km) a day.

Its main food is snakes, which it kills by kicking them in the head with its talons, but it also eats a wide range of other ground dwellers, including rats and insects.

Which Wasp Makes a Spider Spin It a Cocoon?

There is a Costa Rican wasp, called *Hymenoepimecis argyraphaga*, that has an amazing way of getting its cocoon built. The process starts when the female wasp approaches a *Plesiometa argyra* spider. This is an enormous, fearsome spider that most insects sensibly avoid, but not this one. Instead, the wasp hovers in front of the spider and then lands directly on it. Then it quickly brings its ovipositor forward and implants an egg on the spider's back before swiftly flying off.

The spider seems to be unharmed, but as the egg develops, it remains on the spider's body, absorbing nutrients from its host. The night before the wasp larva pupates, the spider will destroy her own web. So far this is fairly normal behavior: most web spinners regularly destroy their webs, eating the silk and thus recycling it.

> a female wasp lays her egg on the spider's back

However, the wasp larva has injected the spider with a chemical that makes the spider spin a new web that will be very different from her usual orb web. This web has none of the usual features—

no radial spokes and no sticky spirals. Instead, it is attached to the surrounding plants by extra-strong, reinforced threads. Unknowingly, the spider is building the last web it will ever produce. Once it is completed, the spider sits motionless underneath it and never moves again. The chemical from the wasp larva now kills the spider.

The wasp larva now feasts on the spider's body, eventually dropping the dry, empty husk. At dawn, the wasp spins its own bright orange cocoon, which hangs inside the spider's final web, elevated and protected from ants and Costa Rica's heavy rainstorms.

Can Bugs Act Like Soldiers

Siafu, which are also known as driver ants, Matabele ants, or safari ants, are one of the fiercest and most dangerous of all insects. They are found mainly in Africa, where they live in large colonies. They have enormous jaws and eat a varied diet that includes insects, earthworms, termites, and sometimes even larger animals, including weak or injured mammals.

They travel in raiding parties several hundred strong, marching in columns, about six abreast. Alongside the soldiers run minors, which are about half their size. Earlier, a scout will have laid down a scent trail to lead them to their target, such as a termites' nest. As they march, they "sing" by rubbing a patch of ridges on their front.

When they reach the termite hill, they will be faced by ranks of soldier termites. These are bigger than the siafu, with huge, armored heads and powerful jaws, but nonetheless they are no match for the siafu. The siafu seize the termites and quickly inject their venom into the termites' brains, killing them within seconds. The raiders now start to make a pile of the vanquished termites.

With no guards left, the termite nest is now defenseless. The siafu storm inside, killing all the soft-bodied worker termites they can find. For a quarter of an hour, the slaughter may continue as the pile of bodies grows. The minors now start to carry the bodies back to their nest, carrying as many as six at a time. Eventually, the army marches back home, this time singing a different song, presumably a triumphant song of victory.

Which Bird Attacks in Squadrons

Fieldfares are one of the largest members of the thrush family and are found in Europe and northern Asia. They are fairly large birds, around 9 to 10.5 inches (23 to 27 cm) long, which feed on insects, berries, and earthworms. They are sociable birds that often nest together in colonies. Like many birds, they alert one another to the arrival of a predator.

Say a chick stealer such as a magpie comes along. The first fieldfare to spot the threat will give a call, sounding the alarm. Rather than simply rushing for cover, the rest of the birds will take up the cry themselves, so that it quickly becomes an unnerving cacophony. They then dive-bomb the predator, shrieking at it as they swoop down, releasing bombs of feces. Fieldfares are adept at aiming these bombs, and many of them will hit their target. The magpie may soon end up covered in feces, making it fall to the ground, where it will hop away, dejectedly, to clean itself.

Which Crustacean Has a Hidden Switchblade

The mantis shrimp lives in shallow tropical and subtropical seas. Its main claw has a sharp extension that it keeps folded out of sight, a bit like a closed switchblade. When hunting, the mantis shrimp flicks open this claw extension at enormous speed and smashes it into its prey. It is one of the fastest physical movements that any animal is known to produce. A large Californian mantis shrimp, which is about 10 inches (25 cm) long, can have a strike speed of 33 feet (10 m) per second, which is about the speed of a bullet fired from a rifle. This strike is powerful enough to cut small

> a large Californian mantis shrimp can **smash** its main **claw** into its prey at the **speed** of **a bullet**

fish in two or crack open the shells of crabs and shellfish. Mantis shrimps are therefore not recommended as pets because their amazing weapon has been known to crack the side of a double-walled safety-glass fish tank.

Which Crustacean Kidnaps Creatures for Protection?

The resourceful hermit crab uses entire creatures as weapons. A hermit crab will attach a sea anemone to the back of its shell. Sea anemones have vicious, stinging tentacles, which serve to keep any predators far away from the hermit crab.

The little boxer crab takes this innovation even further. It carries a small anemone in each of its two front pincers and brandishes them like swords. If any predator threatens the crab, it thrusts its pincers forward, wielding its two bunches of stinging tentacles. The crab never lets go of its anemones, which means it is unable to use its front pincers to pass food into its mouth as most crabs do. Instead, it has learned to use its two front legs for this purpose.

Which Worm Captures Its Prey by Covering It with Glue?

The answer is the velvet worm, which, in fact, is not even a worm. It looks a bit like a caterpillar, with a long, segmented body and between 13 and 43 pairs of stumpy feet. Velvet worms are usually around 2 inches (5 cm) long and are found in most tropical climates. However, they are very wary creatures and avoid light, so they are rarely seen. They have a fascinating evolutionary history. They are believed to have existed largely unchanged for 500 million years and may represent an evolutionary link between arthropods—that's the group that includes insects and spiders—and annelids, such as earthworms.

Velvet worms tend to live in dark, damp, secluded places such as caves, rotting logs, and leaf litter. They are cute, colorful creatures, but they are also voracious predators. They hunt at night, often killing prey much larger than themselves, including crickets, termites, wood lice, and spiders. The worms capture their prey by covering it in a sticky glue, which they shoot from two powerful tubes next to their mouth. Velvet worms can fire this glue up to 1 foot (about 30 cm). As the glue flies, it dries in the air before entangling the unfortunate victim, leaving it unable to escape. Now the worm will bite into its prey, injecting it with saliva that softens and liquefies the meal so it's ready to be devoured. The velvet worm will also eat the glue, which is rich in protein.

> **velvet worms can fire glue up to one foot**

6
Weird Wonders

Why Do Penguins Look So Funny?

Penguins are naturally comic creatures that manage to be simultaneously cute and absurd-looking. But what is the reason for their unmistakable black-and-white feathers?

Well, it may look a little daft on land, but a penguin's coat is extremely practical. First, it protects the bird from its predators—sharks, killer whales, and seals, each of which can pose a threat only in the water. A penguin's coat helps to camouflage it while it swims. From above, its black back is hard to make out against the darkness of the ocean. From below, its white front is hard to pick out against the white of the sky.

The penguin's distinctive coloring is also useful for managing the bird's temperature, which is of vital importance for a creature living in the frozen Antarctic. When a penguin is cold, it will turn its black back to the sun to soak up as much of the sun's warmth as possible. When the penguin gets too hot, as unlikely as this may sound, it can turn its white belly to the sun to reflect the heat.

Why Don't Woodpeckers Get Headaches

Woodpeckers hunt for insects that few other birds can reach, hidden beneath the bark of trees. They do this by pecking at the bark with great force: each blow hits the tree at around 25 miles (40 km) per hour, and they peck up to 20 times per second. These blows are so powerful that if the bird's beak were not locked together by a special clasp, the two mandibles would fly apart.

A single one of these powerful whacks could knock the woodpecker unconscious if its force were to reach the bird's brain, but luckily the woodpecker's head is cleverly designed to cushion the blow. Woodpeckers have muscles at the base of their beak that act as shock absorbers. Furthermore, woodpeckers' brains are very small and suspended in fluid. Consequently, none of the impact reaches the brain, and so the woodpecker remains conscious.

Woodpeckers also have clever ways to protect themselves from flying splinters. Their nostrils are tiny slits that are protected by special feathers. And to stop splinters from getting in their eyes, woodpeckers close special membranes over their eyes a millisecond before each peck hits the wood.

Which Bird Can See Even with Its Eyes Closed

The potoo is an enormous bird that can reach more than 19 inches (0.5 m) in height and is found in the American tropics. Despite its size, even in broad daylight a potoo is almost impossible to see because it has amazing camouflage. The bird usually perches on top of a tree stump. It has brown, mottled feathers, which blend in perfectly with the tree's bark. If a predator approaches, the potoo takes further steps to make itself invisible.

It lowers its tail, pressing it flat against the bark of the stump so that there is no visible joint. It then lifts its head so that its beak is pointing vertically, making it look just like the broken end of branch, and closes its eyes.

Closing its eyes suggests that the potoo has considerable confidence in its camouflage. It will even stay completely still when a predator gets within 3 feet (1 m) of it. However, although its eyelids are shut, the bird can still see faintly because its eyelids have two tiny vertical slits. They let through just enough light for the potoo to keep an eye on any approaching threat. If a predator does get too close for the potoo's comfort, it will suddenly take off and fly away. It must make quite a startling sight to see a broken tree stump suddenly take flight!

> It must make quite a **startling** sight to see a broken **tree stump** suddenly **take flight!**

Which Butterfly Is an Escape Artist ?

The hairstreak butterfly has a false head on its hind wings. The false head distracts birds from the butterfly's actual head and confuses them when the butterfly escapes, seemingly flying backward.

In fact, there are a number of other creatures that have false heads to confuse and deter predators. The shingle-back lizard, for example, has a large, stumpy tail that is exactly the same size and shape as its head.

There is also an amazing type of frog found in Chile, Brazil, and Uruguay that uses its entire body as a false head. The appropriately named four-eyed frog has two large swellings on its sides, which look just like eyes. They sit just above the frog's legs, and the overall effect is that the frog's whole body looks like the head of a much larger, more threatening creature. In addition, these false eyes are actually poison glands, so even if a predator does decide to bite the frog, the unpleasant taste will usually make it let go pretty quickly.

How Does a Snake Swallow an Antelope ?

Snakes are some of the most astonishing predators on earth. There are more than 2,900 species of snake, and all of them are carnivorous hunters despite their apparent lack of advantages. Snakes have no legs to chase their prey with, no hands to grab with, and no teeth with which to chew. Most species of snake can't even see particularly well. And yet they are found on every continent except Antarctica, and they prey on animals many times their size, including cats, pigs, and even antelope. How do they do it?

Most snakes kill their prey in one of three ways. Some use constriction—wrapping their body around the prey, tightening their grip every time the victim exhales until eventually it is unable to breathe in. Some snakes kill using their venom. More often, though, snakes use their venom to paralyze and subdue their prey before swallowing it whole.

Snakes are able to swallow creatures more than three times larger than their own heads, which is somewhat equivalent to our being able to swallow a basketball whole. A snake is able to do this because its skin and body are extremely elastic, and its skeleton doesn't limit the size of food that can be passed down its body. Snakes can also open their jaws to as much as 130 degrees, whereas the human jaw can reach a maximum angle of only 30 degrees. Also, a snake's lower jaw has two halves, left and right, which are connected by a flexible, elastic ligament, allowing them to be stretched apart.

snakes are able to swallow creatures more than three times larger than their own heads

Snakes have no teeth to chew with, so they have to swallow their food whole. They swallow their prey headfirst because creatures such as birds, hedgehogs, and goats have feathers, spines, and horns, which could provide resistance or cause injury if ingested the wrong way around. Snakes have strong cheek and throat muscles with which they push their prey down to the stomach in a process that can take several hours.

Once the food reaches the stomach, the process of digestion can begin. If the meal is a big one, digestion can take a long time. Sudden movements may be risky if the meal includes spiky things such as spines, claws, or horns, so the snake will now try to lie low, out of the way, moving as little as possible.

A large meal will cause the snake's body to undergo substantial changes to facilitate the process of digestion and storage. Its heart will swell by 40 percent, and its liver may double in size. It can take more than a week for a snake to digest a large meal. Then, when digestion is finally completed, the snake's internal systems enter a dormant state, with significantly reduced functions, to conserve energy.

In this way, snakes can swallow creatures many

times their size. An African rock python was once observed swallowing a 130-pound (59-kg) antelope. There are also reports of snakes swallowing alligators whole and even human beings. In one recent example, in Indonesia, an entire human body, covered in slime and digestive juices, was said to have been cut out of a python.

Which Frog Has a Visible, Beating Heart

A tiny frog called the glass frog is found in many parts of Central and South Americas. Glass frogs range from around 1 to 3 inches (3 to 8 cm) in length and look a bit like tree frogs, with attractive lime-green skin on their backs. But if you turn the frog over, you will see something quite astonishing. The skin of the glass frog's front is transparent, allowing you to see its internal organs at work: its liver, digestive tract, even its beating heart and circulating blood.

Which Tadpole Changes Shape to Foil Its Predator ?

There is a species of frog called *Rana pirica* whose tadpoles have evolved a unique way of protecting themselves from predators. The tadpoles can sense whether or not their predators, which are salamander larvae, are nearby. If the tadpoles sense the presence of a predator, they transform themselves into a different, bulging body shape, which makes them too big for the salamander larvae to fit into their mouths. Then if the predators leave, the tadpoles will return to their normal size.

However, the salamander larvae have developed an equally impressive response. If they sense the presence of the *Rana pirica* tadpoles, the salamander larvae will also change their shape, with their heads becoming much broader, allowing them to swallow the enlarged tadpoles.

Which Insect Grows
a Fake Ant on Its Back ?

Dangerous creatures tend to have distinctive markings because it is important that they be recognized as dangerous. Honeybees, for example, carry a sting that can be deadly for many of their potential predators. However, if it is forced to actually use its sting, the bee itself will die. Therefore, the bee has a distinctive black-and-yellow pattern, colors that are understood in nature to indicate poison, to scare predators away. Similarly, the poison-dart frogs of the Amazon have bright, colorful skins, which indicate that they are among the most poisonous creatures on the planet.

However, if this strategy works, then it opens up the possibility of mimicry. If looking like a bee is enough to keep predators away, then why should a creature actually bother to develop a poisonous sting, which costs considerable resources and energy? Thus, while bees, wasps, and hornets are actually dangerous, there are also numerous other insects that look just like them, but in fact carry no sting at all. For them, just looking dangerous is enough.

for some, just looking dangerous is enough

This mimicry is developed to an extreme degree by a small treehopper called *Heteronotus*, which is found in the forests of Central America. This bug has evolved with a full-scale model of an ant on its back. If you look at it from above, as a bird would do, all you will see is the black shape of an ant, with gaping jaws, a thin waist, and a black abdomen. Beneath this imitation is the treehopper itself, which has a normal treehopper abdomen and wings and looks in all other respects just like an average member of its family. Looking like an ant protects the treehopper from birds, for birds generally avoid eating ants because they taste awful, they have a hard exoskeleton, and they often sting or bite.

Why Do Zebras Have Stripes?

The reason why zebras have their distinctive stripes is one of nature's most enduring mysteries. Even today we are still not exactly sure, although a number of theories have been proposed. One long-standing theory holds that this pattern works as camouflage, breaking up the outline of the zebra on the open savannas of Africa, where it roams. Many scientists are far from convinced by this for the simple reason that zebras are quite eye-catching and do not seem to be well camouflaged at all. However, the zebra's main predator, the lion, is color-blind. So it is possible that the zebra's vertical stripes do camouflage it in tall grass, even though to our eyes its coloration may make it appear obvious.

Another theory suggests that the zebra's alternating bands of black and white stripes reflect heat in different ways, creating cooling currents of air over the zebra's body. Yet another theory proposes that the stripes confuse the visual system of the bloodsucking tsetse fly. At least one function does seem to have been convincingly demonstrated. Zebras' stripes vary significantly from one individual animal to another, and it's clear that the zebras do identify and remember other members of the group by these distinctive markings.

zebras' **stripes** vary significantly from one **individual** animal to another, and zebras **identify** and **remember** other members of the group by these distinctive **markings**

Coming up...

snakes fart

7
Extra-Disgusting Details

Sniff

Sniff

Sniff

Which Frog Coughs Up
Its Entire Stomach?

When they need to vomit, some frogs have an incredible technique. Instead of simply expelling the stomach's contents, as we do, they cough up their entire stomach. Then they carefully rinse it out with their right hand, push it back inside, and swallow it. Why do they always rinse it with their right hand rather than their left? Apparently, it is because the tissues that hold the stomach in place are shorter on the right side, which means that when the frog expels its stomach, it always hangs to the right, where it can be washed only by the right hand.

Do Snakes Fart?

Snakes scare off potential predators in a number of ways. They hiss at them, raise themselves up, puff up their bodies, or rattle their tails. Two types of North American snakes have another way of scaring off their enemies. The Sonoran coral snake and the western hooknose snake are both quite small, which makes it harder for them to be physically imposing. Instead, they fart, although the technical term is the rather more proper "cloacal popping." Each "pop" lasts for less than two-tenths of a second and may be repeated several times. Relative to their size, these snakes fart quite loudly: the farts can be heard up to around 6 feet (2 m) away and sound just like our own farts, although slightly higher-pitched.

the **technical term** for a **snake fart** is a **"cloacal pop"**

This may be why the farts are effective: they sound like the farts of animals large enough to scare off the snake's usual predators. In tests, the snakes were found to fart only when threatened. They do so using two sets of muscles to isolate a compressed bubble of air, and then release it to the outside in an explosive burst. Apparently, they sometimes put so much force into these farts that they fling themselves up off the ground!

Why Does the Australian Rainbow Pitta Decorate Its Nest with Wallaby Poo ?

The rainbow pitta is an attractive and colorful Australian bird that is known as the "jewel of the forest." It is similar in size and shape to a thrush, reaching about 8 inches (20 cm) in length. It has a velvet black head and breast, with green upper parts and an electric-blue patch on its wing. The pitta is found in the steamy rain forests and tropical mangrove and eucalyptus forests of northern Australia, where it lives on a diet of snails, worms, and insects.

Rainbow pittas are shy, sensitive birds that are difficult to observe. They breed at the beginning of the rainy season, between October and March. They usually build their nests in trees but will also nest on clumps of bamboo, in thickets, on tree stumps, or even on the ground. Their nests are made of twigs and leaves, in the shape of a football. The interior of the nest is lined with fine leaves and is reached via an entrance hole in the side of the dome. Next to this entrance, the rainbow pitta will often lay a kind of doormat, which it makes out of wallaby poo.

As you can imagine, a doormat made of poop in a tropical climate can get a bit stinky, but the bird doesn't seem to mind. In fact, the stink seems to be the point. In the forests where the rainbow pitta is found, brown tree snakes are a significant threat. These snakes will eat the bird's eggs if they can find the nest, and they use their powerful sense of smell to search for them. Decorating their nests with pungent wallaby poo, which they collect from the forest floor, fools the rainbow pittas' slithering predators and protects their young.

> a **doormat** made of **poop** in a **tropical** climate can get a bit **stinky**

Which Bird Kills Its Enemies by Throwing Up on Them?

The fulmar is a large seabird that looks a lot like a seagull. The name *fulmar* means "foul gull," and the name is well deserved, because the fulmar's main mode of defense is to vomit disgusting yellow oil over its enemies. This vomit is not only unpleasant and smelly but also potentially lethal. Most of the fulmar's predators are birds of prey, including skuas, ospreys, and sea eagles. The fulmar's vomit sticks to their feathers, making them unable to fly. It can even cause them to drown.

In fulmar families, both parents go hunting at sea for up to 20 hours at a time, leaving their nests undefended. The chicks are obviously not strong enough to defend themselves against birds of prey in a conventional manner, but fulmar chicks are born with this amazing ability to vomit oil and to aim it with precision. At just four days old, they can puke as far as 18 inches (0.5 m), while older chicks can spew three times that distance. When they are born, the chicks even instinctively vomit at their parents until they learn to recognize them as family.

Why Are Penguins Such Powerful Pooers?

penguins' poop power is four times greater than a **human** being's

A group of European scientists recently conducted a study of penguin feces and found that the birds could expel their poop with a force of up to 60 kilopascals (a pascal is a unit of pressure)—four times greater than a human being's equivalent poop power. Furthermore, the penguins could expel their poop to a distance of 16 inches (41 cm).

It seems that the penguin has developed this unusual talent in order to avoid soiling its feathers or its nest. For this unusual research, the scientists in question were awarded an Ig Nobel Prize, which is a lighthearted science prize designed to honor scientific achievements that "make people laugh—then think."

Penguins are not the only power pooers out

there. Kingfishers and hornbills will back up to the entrance of their waterside tree hole to expel a stream directly into the river; the stream will usually be powerful enough to avoid leaving any streak or mark on the tree or the riverbank. This helps them avoid detection by predators. If their tree were marked with feces, their hole would be easily discovered.

One reason why birds are able to develop such a gift is that they produce their urine and feces in one single stream, making it runnier than the excrement of mammals. This technique not only protects the birds from detection by predators but also keeps their nests clean, limiting the risk of infection and disease.

Which Bird Disguises Itself as a Pile of Cow Dung?

The nacunda nighthawk lives out on the open plains of Brazil. It is nocturnal and spends most of its days resting on the ground. There are no trees or bushes in which to hide from predators, so the bird seems to be completely exposed. But it has developed a cunning form of camouflage. When it crouches, it looks like a pile of unappetizing cow dung.

The curious thing about this is that cows are a fairly recent addition to the wildlife of Brazil. There were no cows in Brazil until just a few centuries ago, when they were introduced by European explorers. And there are no other large grazing mammals on the plains of Brazil that might produce something similar to cow poo. This raises a fascinating question: How did the nacunda nighthawk evolve to resemble a pile of cow poo if there were no cows around to produce poop for it to mimic? It could not have evolved this talent in just a few centuries.

Scientists do have a theory to explain this. Although there are no other large grazing mammals on the plains today, once upon a time there were. Around a thousand years ago, these grasslands were the home of giant sloths and great armadillos, which were the size of today's cows. These creatures have been extinct for centuries, but the fact of their existence raises the amazing possibility that the nacunda nighthawk's camouflage may actually be providing us with an accurate picture of what their dung looked like all those centuries ago.

Why Do Vultures Poop on Themselves?

Staying cool is a difficult art to master. The only animals with sweat glands are mammals, and not all mammals have them (cats, whales, and rodents, for example, have lost most or all of their sweat glands).

Birds lose heat by raising their down feathers to increase airflow to the skin. They also take baths and pant. Some birds, including vultures, also do something fairly disgusting to keep their temperature down: they urinate and defecate down their legs.

Birds have a single posterior opening called a cloaca, which means that their waste products all come out together. (This is why bird poop is often so runny, because it also contains the bird's urine.) It may sound gross, but this habit probably also helps keep the birds clean. Bird poop contains uric acid, which is an antiseptic. Having it on its own legs may therefore help keep a vulture free from germs after it has walked through a carcass.

Some cranes and storks approach the problem of temperature regulation in a slightly different way. Their chicks are reared on stick platforms in tropical climates, where the heat of the sun can be very damaging. To keep them cool, parents collect stomachfuls of water and vomit over their young, giving them a refreshing shower. Herons solve this problem in an even more unpleasant way—they simply poop over their young.

Which Insect Lives Off of Cows' Runny Noses?

This is the rather unpleasant diet of the face fly, or *Musca autumnalis*. Face flies are found throughout most of North America, Europe, and Asia and are a major pest for cattle and horses.

Face flies hibernate over the winter and then emerge in the spring. The females lay their eggs in fresh manure, and these eggs usually hatch within 24 hours. The maggots grow in stages while feeding on the manure and then move to nearby soil for the final stage of their development. Depending on the local temperature, an adult fly will emerge in about two to three weeks.

Adult face flies live and feed on cattle, dining mainly on the animal's facial secretions, including tears, nasal mucus, sweat, and saliva. They have abrasive, spongy mouthparts, which soak up these protein-rich secretions and also cause the animal's eyes to produce more tears, which in turn attract more face flies. They are not considered to be blood feeders because their mouthparts are not able to pierce the host's skin. But given the chance, they will feed on a wound opened up by other blood-feeding flies.

We humans suffer from a very similar pest. The

eye gnat is a type of tiny fly, less than a tenth of an inch (2 mm) in length, that is found in many hot climates, including the southern United States. In the summer, annoying eye gnats congregate around our eyes and noses to feed on the moisture.

Which Type of Ant Loves Hospitals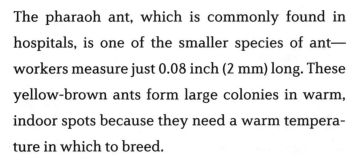

The pharaoh ant, which is commonly found in hospitals, is one of the smaller species of ant—workers measure just 0.08 inch (2 mm) long. These yellow-brown ants form large colonies in warm, indoor spots because they need a warm temperature in which to breed.

They particularly thrive in hospitals because they like to eat a diet rich in protein, and so they feast on bloody bandages, dressings, IV solution, and surgical wounds. They are trail-making ants that can communicate information about new sources of food and water to one another, which helps the population to spread. Because they seek out sources of water, they will often find their way to toilets, drains, and bedpans. This makes them a serious health risk because they can transmit diseases, infect food, and contaminate sterile materials.

What Happens at a Dung Beetle Wedding?

Dung beetles love one thing above all others: poop. When a dung beetle finds a tempting pile of droppings, it sifts through it, looking for the best morsels. Having made its selections, the beetle will then start to roll its dung into a ball, which soon becomes considerably bigger than the beetle itself. It can roll a ball that is 50 times its own weight by climbing on top and manipulating it with its legs.

Skillful beetles can roll their dungball at speeds of up to about 46 feet (14 m) a minute. They need to travel quickly because dung is a precious commodity. Other dung beetles may well come along and try to steal it. To minimize the risk of being robbed, dung beetles will always travel in a straight line toward their burial hole. Amazingly, they navigate by using polarized light from the moon. With luck, the beetle will manage to bring its prize home to a safe burial spot, ready to provide a delicious source of food for many days.

Yet there is more to dung than just a delicious meal. Every aspect of dung beetle society revolves around poo. A male dung beetle will often woo a female by presenting her with a ball of dung. Together, the couple then roll the ball back to their new home, with him pushing and her pulling, in a bizarre kind of wedding ceremony. The female will then lay her eggs inside the dung ball, which provides an abundant source of food for their growth before the young eventually eat their way out.

> a male dung beetle will often **WOO** a female by presenting her with a **ball of dung**

Why Do Birds
Rub Ants into Their Feathers ?

Most animals that accidentally disturb a wood ants' nest soon come to regret it because the worker ants swarm out in an angry mob, squirting jets of acid at them from glands at the end of their abdomen. This is enough to repel most creatures, but some birds deliberately land on ants' nests and invite them to squirt.

Jays, starlings, and crows all enjoy sitting on ants' nests, in a process called "anting." As the angry ants swarm over them, the birds will fluff up their feathers, letting the ants discharge acid into every crevice. Some even pick up ants in their beaks and rub them over their feathers, as if squeezing out as much acid as they can get. The reason they do this is that the acid cleans the birds' feathers and rids them of any fleas, lice, or other skin parasites they might have picked up. Yet anting does not seem to be a purely functional chore. Many birds look like they enjoy it, cocking their heads back and closing their eyes, as if thrilled by the invigorating sting of the acid.

Birds are not the only creatures that enjoy the attentions of a raging ant swarm. Tortoises can't reach the top of their shells, making it impossible for them to remove any ticks or parasites that may have climbed on board. The North American wood tortoise uses ants to help keep it clean. It will simply walk into the ants' nest and sit still while the insects swarm all over it, squirting antimicrobial acid and killing any parasites they may come across.

Which Beetle Fires Really Smelly Stuff from Its Backside?

The pinacate beetle is a mean-looking black beetle that can reach up to around 1.5 inches (4 cm) in length. It is extremely hardy and is found in great numbers in the deserts of Mexico and the southwestern United States, where few other creatures can survive. Pinacate beetles even have a mountain range named after them, the Pinacate Mountains, on the border between Sonora (Mexico) and Arizona.

Pinacate beetles are also known as clown beetles because they do something bizarre when faced with danger. Rather than run away, these beetles will hurriedly stand on their head, often tumbling over into a somersault if they fail to balance properly. A beetle may flip over a number of times before settling into a controlled headstand. Although this display is entertaining, it's wise to take it as a warning. If the beetle continues to feel threatened, it may attack by shooting a disgusting, noxious chemical from its rear end, which it can fire up to about 30 inches (76 cm). For this reason, pinacate beetles have another nickname: they are also commonly known as stink beetles. This substance can cause painful burning and temporary blindness if it gets into your eyes, and it is extremely difficult to wash off.

However, a number of predators have figured out a

> when faced with **danger**, pinacate beetles will hurriedly stand on **their head**

way to take advantage of the stink beetle's abundance. Grasshopper mice teach their young to grab the beetle and stick its rear end into the ground, where it can't do any harm. Then they chew through the top half of the beetle. The beetle's other predators include burrowing owls, loggerhead shrikes, and, appropriately enough, skunks.

Why Do Hedgehogs Spit on Themselves?

Surprisingly, perhaps, given their prickly appearance, hedgehogs are regarded as one of the animal kingdom's cutest creatures. However, they have one very disgusting habit. A hedgehog will chew on the toxic skin of a toad, which produces poisonous foam, and then contort its body to spit the foaming saliva all over its own back. It's not clear why it does this, but presumably the foam is useful for deterring predators.

This habit may also help to explain how hedgehogs have developed such incredible immunity to poison. Hedgehogs can survive a bite from an adder, which would kill a guinea pig in five minutes. Also, it takes more chloroform to knock out a hedgehog than any other creature of similar size.

How Does the Brown Hyena Communicate Using Its Rear End

In the Kalahari Desert, brown hyenas are constantly marking their territory, and they do this by a complex system of smelly deposits. They live in clans of about a dozen and travel long distances looking for food, which for the brown hyena consists of dead animal flesh and sometimes small mammals. Every few minutes, the hyena will "mark" by straddling a clump of grass and smearing it with oil from a gland near its rear end.

Other mammals mark their territory in a similar way, including civets, but the hyena's system has two parts. They produce a white paste that forms a small bead on the grass and an even smaller blob of black oil that sticks just above it. These two markers serve two very different functions. The white bead is a sign of ownership, warning hyenas of other clans that this territory is taken. This bead holds onto its powerful smell for several weeks. The black bead, on the other hand, is intended as a message for other members of the hyena's own clan. It loses its smell very quickly and vanishes within a few hours. If this bead's smell is strong, it lets any passing hyena know that this territory was patrolled recently and probably doesn't have any food left. If the scent is barely there or gone, the area might be ripe for hunting again. In any single clan's territory, there may be up to 15,000 of these whiffy signposts, and they are frequently updated.

How Do Rhinos Mark Their Territory

With poop, and lots of it! Some animals eat their dung; others bury it, hide it, or present it to their partner as a gift. But rhinos put it on display, in enormous piles more than 1 yard (about 1 m) across. Rhinos use these

rhinos put their poop on display

to mark the boundaries of their territory and may have as many as 30 piles dotted around, each of which they try to visit every day.

These piles serve two useful purposes. First, they notify rival rhinos that this territory is taken, warning them not to trespass. Second, they help the owner of the territory keep its bearings. Rhinos have very poor eyesight, so it's difficult for them to recognize landmarks. However, their sense of smell is excellent, so these dung piles serve as helpful olfactory markers.

Why Do Sloths Turn Green

Sloths are medium-size mammals, usually about 20 inches (about 0.5 m) long, which live in the treetops in rain forests of Central and South Americas. The local tribes in Ecuador refer to sloths using three rather unkind names: *rittor*, *rit*, and *ridette*, which derive from the local words for "sleep," "eat," and "dirty." It's true that sloths do little more than eat and sleep, and they spend their lives hanging upside down from the branches of the trees in which they live. This is because their diet of leaves is very low in nutrients, so they have to expend as little energy as possible. Consequently, sloths have a much lower body temperature and metabolic rate than other mammals of a similar size.

The third accusation, that sloths are dirty, is sadly also true. A sloth's fur is a kind of yellowy-brown when the sloth is young, but as it gets older, its fur gradually turns green. This green color comes from a kind of algae that grows on the sloth's fur. Turning green is useful for the sloths. It helps camouflage them in the treetops, making it harder for predators to see them. The algae also contains lots of beneficial nutrients, so the sloth will frequently be seen snacking on lumps from its fur.

Which Bird Mugs Other Birds for Their Vomit?

The magnificent frigate bird is found around the coast of Australia and the Pacific islands. The *magnificent* in its name refers to is size—its wing-span is an enormous 6 feet, 6 inches (2 m)—but it could also describe the bird's aerial skills. The frig-ate bird is an amazing acrobat that can skim the surface of the sea to snatch fish using its hooked beak.

It also has another way of hunting that isn't ex-actly magnificent: it mugs other birds in flight to steal their vomit. The frigate bird can tell when another bird is flying home after a successful fishing mission. It will attack this bird in flight, perhaps tugging on its tail feathers. The victim, often a booby, will be knocked off balance and throw up its catch. The frigate bird then swoops into a dive and catches the regurgitated fish be-fore it hits the water.

In Mexico, the aplomado falcon is another aerial pirate. Like the frigate bird, it is quite ca-pable of catching its own prey, but studies have found that its odds of success are greater if it sim-ply steals from other birds. Researchers found

that the falcon's piracy attempts were successful 82 percent of the time, while actually trying
to hunt for food itself produced positive results
only 38 percent of the time.

Why Do Frogs Eat Their Own Skin

Frogs have soft, delicate skin that wears away
quickly and has to be frequently replaced. Many
frogs shed their skin as often as once a week. The
process begins with a lot of twisting, bending,
and stretching to loosen the old skin. The outer
layer becomes separated from the new skin growing underneath and begins to split. The frog will
scratch to loosen the outer layer with its forelegs,
as if pulling off a scab (it may well itch and annoy the frog, just like a scab). At some point, the
frog will be able to get part of the skin in its mouth,
and then it will gradually pull the whole thing
into its mouth, still loosening it with its legs, until the whole skin has been swallowed. Disgusting

though this may sound, growing a new skin takes a lot of energy and nutrients, and so this way the frog gets to recycle the old skin. So you see, it's true: frogs really are green!

Which Creature Eats with Its Eyes ?

This is not a trick question. Frogs and toads put their eyes to work as they eat, and not only to watch out for threats or more food passing by. So how does it work? Well, they don't use their eyes as a mouth. They don't chew with them or ingest food through them. Instead, they use their eyes to push their food down into their stomach when they swallow. When a frog eats a tasty morsel, such as a small cricket, it will close its eyes and retract its eyeballs into its body. These push into the frog's pharynx, against the cricket, and repeated pushes gradually force the food down to the back of the frog's esophagus.

Why Do Dogs Eat Poop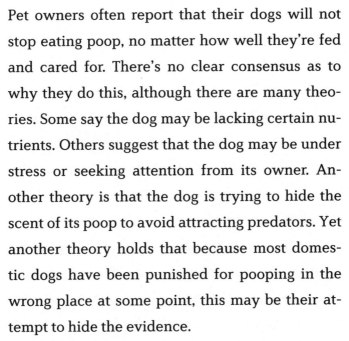

Pet owners often report that their dogs will not stop eating poop, no matter how well they're fed and cared for. There's no clear consensus as to why they do this, although there are many theories. Some say the dog may be lacking certain nutrients. Others suggest that the dog may be under stress or seeking attention from its owner. Another theory is that the dog is trying to hide the scent of its poop to avoid attracting predators. Yet another theory holds that because most domestic dogs have been punished for pooping in the wrong place at some point, this may be their attempt to hide the evidence.

There may be no conclusive answer yet, but we do know that eating poop is not confined to dogs. A great number of animal species regularly eat their own poop, including rabbits, Japanese hares, northern pika, sportive lemurs, koalas, possums, chinchillas, European beavers, guinea pigs, and Norway lemmings.

Rabbits routinely eat their own leavings—for them it's simply one stage of the digestive process. A rabbit's diet consists of grass, leaves, and other plant matter. This is a diet that is low in nutrients and difficult to digest. To ensure that they are getting as much energy and nutrition out of their food as possible, rabbits eat their poop as soon as it emerges. This lets the rabbit's stomach give the food a second digestive processing. The round dry pellets that you see in a rabbit warren are what's left after the rabbit has digested its food twice.

Other animals are believed to eat their poop for a rather different reason. Many bird species are particularly careful about hiding their poop for fear of alerting predators to the location of their nest. In the first few days of their life, the chicks of many bird species produce feces enclosed in a gelatinous sac. Their parents will swallow this, which suggests that the poop may retain some nutri-

a great **number** of animal species regularly **eat** their own **poop**

tional value that the chick's undeveloped stomach was unable to process. As the chick gets older, the parent bird will stop eating its feces and instead carry them away to be dumped.

the end

Acknowledgments

We would like to thank our wonderful, dedicated literary agent, Andrew Lownie, for making this book happen. We also thank our editor, Andrew John, for professionalism and attention to detail that have gone a long way to covering up our own deficiencies in these areas. Many thanks to Claudia Dyer and Helen Stanton at Piatkus and Sara Carder, Andrew Yackira, and all the team at Tarcher. Finally, we thank our families for their continuing patience, support, and encouragement.

For more kid-tastic facts, look for

Why Fish Fart

Gross but True Things

You'll Wish You Didn't Know

Dewey

Dewey

the Library Cat:
A True Story

Vicki Myron

with

Bret Witter

SCHOLASTIC INC.
New York Toronto London Auckland
Sydney Mexico City New Delhi Hong Kong

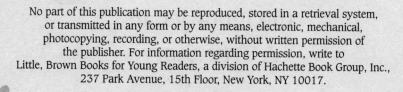

ISBN 978-0-545-46204-4

12 11 10 9 8 7 6 5 4   12 13 14 15 16 17/0

Printed in the U.S.A.   40

First Scholastic printing, April 2012

Vicki—To Dewey, my Little Buddy

Bret—To Lydia and Isaac, as always

CONTENTS

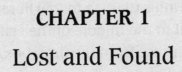

CHAPTER 1

Lost and Found

You find all kinds of things in a library book return box—garbage, snowballs, soda cans. Stick a hole in a wall and you're asking for trouble. I should know. My name is Vicki Myron, and I am the former director of the Spencer Public Library in Spencer, Iowa. At our library, the book return slot was in a back alley across the street from the town's middle school, so rocks and snowballs were the least of our worries. Several times we were startled in the middle of the day by a loud explosion from the back of the library. Inside the book return box, we'd find a firecracker.

After the weekend, the drop box would also be full of books, so every Monday morning I took them out of the box and loaded them onto one of our book carts. Same thing every week. Until one morning, one of the coldest mornings of the year, when I came in with the book cart and found Jean Hollis Clark, a fellow librarian, standing dead still in the middle of the staff room.

"I heard a noise from the drop box," Jean said.

"What kind of noise?"

"I think it's an animal."

"A what?"

"An animal," Jean said. "I think there's an animal in the drop box."

That was when I heard it, a low rumble from under the metal cover. It didn't sound like an animal. It sounded like an old man clearing his throat.

Gurr-gug-gug. Gurr-gug-gug.

But the opening at the top of the chute was only a few inches wide, so that would be quite a squeeze for an old man. It had to be an animal. But what kind? I got down on my knees, reached over to the lid, and hoped for a chipmunk.

What I got instead was a blast of freezing air. The night before, the temperature had reached minus fifteen degrees, and that didn't take into account the wind, which cut under your coat and squeezed your bones. And on that night, of all nights, someone had jammed a book into the return slot, wedging it open. It was as cold in the box as it was outside, maybe colder, since the box was lined with metal. It was the kind of cold that made it almost painful to breathe.

I was still catching my breath, in fact, when I saw the kitten huddled in the front left corner of the box. It was tucked up in a little space underneath a book, so all I could see at first was its head. It looked gray in the shadows, almost like a little rock, and I could tell its fur was dirty and tangled. Carefully, I lifted the book. The kitten looked up at me, slowly and sadly, and for a second I looked straight into its huge golden eyes. Then it lowered its head and sank down into its hole.

At that moment, I lost every bone in my body and just melted.

The kitten wasn't trying to appear tough. It wasn't trying to hide. I don't even think it was scared. It was just hoping to be saved.

I lifted the kitten out of the box. It was so small that my hands nearly swallowed it. We found out later it was eight weeks old, but it looked like it was barely eight days old. It was so thin I could see every rib. I could feel its heart beating, its lungs pumping. The poor kitten was so weak it could barely hold up its head, and it was shaking uncontrollably. It opened its mouth, but the sound was weak and ragged.

And the cold! That's what I remember most, because I couldn't believe a living animal could be so cold. It felt like there was no warmth at all. So I cradled the kitten in my arms to share my heat. It didn't fight. Instead, it snuggled into my chest and laid its head against my heart.

"Oh, my," said Jean.

"The poor baby," I said, squeezing tighter.

Neither of us said anything for a while. We were just staring at the kitten.

Finally Jean broke the silence. "How do you think it got in there?"

I wasn't thinking about last night. I was only thinking about right now. It was too early to call the veterinarian, who wouldn't be in for an hour. But the kitten was so cold. Even in the warmth of my arms, I could feel it shaking.

"We've got to do something," I said.

Jean grabbed a towel, and we wrapped the little fellow up until only its pink nose was sticking out. Its huge beautiful eyes were staring from the shadows.

"Let's give it a warm bath," I said. "Maybe that will stop the shivering."

I filled the staff room sink with warm water, testing it with my elbow as I clutched the kitten in my arms. It slid into the sink like a block of ice. Jean found some shampoo in the art closet, and I rubbed the kitten slowly and lovingly. As the water turned grayer and grayer, the kitten's wild shivering turned to soft purring. I smiled. This kitten was tough. But it was so very young. When I finally lifted it out of the sink, it looked like a newborn: huge lidded eyes and big ears sticking out from a tiny head. Wet, scared, and meowing quietly for its mother.

We dried it with the blow-dryer we used for drying glue at craft time. Within thirty seconds, I was holding a beautiful, long-haired orange tabby. The kitten had been so filthy before, I had thought it was gray.

By this time there were four people in the staff room, each cooing over the kitten. Eight hands touched it, seemingly at once. The other three staffers talked over one another while I stood silently cradling the kitten like a baby and rocking back and forth.

"Where did it come from?"

"The drop box."

"No!"

"Is it a boy or a girl?"

I glanced up. They were all looking at me. "A boy," I said.

"He's beautiful."

"How old is he?"

"How did he get in the box?"

I wasn't listening. I only had eyes for the kitten.

"It's so cold."

"Bitterly cold."

"The coldest morning of the year."

A pause, then: "Someone must have put him in the box."

"That's awful."

"Maybe they were trying to save him."

"I don't know. He's so...helpless."

"He's so young."

"He's so beautiful. Oh, he's breaking my heart."

I put him down on the table. The poor kitten could barely stand. The pads on all four of his paws were frostbitten, and over the next week they would turn white and peel off. And yet the kitten managed to do something truly amazing. He steadied himself on the table and slowly looked up into each face. Then he began to hobble. As each librarian reached to pet him, he rubbed his tiny head against her hand and purred. It was as if he wanted to personally thank every person he met for saving his life.

By now it had been twenty minutes since I had pulled the tiny kitten out of the box, and I'd had plenty of time to think through a few things— the once common practice of keeping library cats, my plan to make the library more friendly, the logistics of bowls and food and cat litter, the trusting expression on the kitten's face when he burrowed into my chest and looked up into my eyes. So I was more than prepared when someone finally asked, "What should we do with him?"

"Well," I said, as if the thought had just occurred to me, "maybe we can keep him."

CHAPTER 2

It's a Boy!

The most amazing thing about the kitten was how happy he was that first day. Here he was in a new environment, surrounded by eager strangers who wanted nothing more than to squeeze him, cuddle him, and coo, and he was perfectly calm. No matter how many times we passed him from hand to hand, and no matter what position we held him in, he was never jumpy or fidgety. He never tried to bite or get away. Instead, he just relaxed into each person's arms and stared up into her eyes.

Can you imagine it, the tiniest ball of fluff in the world, no bigger than a juice box, staring up into your eyes with love? And then nuzzling you with his wet nose. And laying his head on your arm. And purring. No wonder we didn't want to put him down! All we wanted to do was grab him, hold him, and love him.

In fact, when I set him down at closing time that first night, I had to watch him for five minutes to make sure he could totter all the way to his food dish and litter box. If he was going to be a library cat, he had to learn to live in the library. If I took him home, even for one night, he might imprint on my home and never want to leave. So I had to leave him alone in the library that first night.

But he looked so tiny as he limped across that big library, like a little lopsided toy. And he looked like he was trying so hard. The poor guy. I don't think his frostbitten feet had touched the ground all day.

Still, I wasn't too worried about him. I'd taken him to the vet that morning, and he wasn't in any health danger. He was an alley cat, so he was used to being alone at night. And thanks to the librarians, he already had a box to sleep in and toys to play with.

One librarian, Doris Armstrong, had even brought him a warm pink blanket. We had all watched as she bent down and scratched the kitten under the chin, then folded the blanket and put it in his cardboard box. The kitten had stepped gingerly into the box, curled his legs underneath his body for warmth, and fallen asleep. And that's exactly where I found him the next morning, asleep on his warm pink blanket.

The next step was to share our little guy with the outside world. The library staff may have already accepted the kitten, but keeping him wasn't our decision. The Spencer Public Library was part of the city government, which meant it answered to the city council and the library board. But it also answered to the ten thousand people of Spencer, and they could be a pretty opinionated bunch. If we wanted to keep the kitten, we needed the library board to approve. But more than that, we needed the town to want him.

As a librarian, I know you can't just put any cute cat in a library. If he's not friendly, he's going to make enemies. If he's too shy or scared, nobody will stand up for him. If he's not patient, he's going to bite. If he's too rambunctious, he's going to make a mess.

I had no doubt about our boy. From the moment he looked up into my eyes, so calm and content, I knew he was perfect for the library. There wasn't a flutter in his heart as I held him in my arms; there wasn't a moment of panic in his eyes. He trusted me completely. He trusted everyone. That's what made him so special: his complete and unabashed trust. And because of it, I trusted him, too.

But that doesn't mean I wasn't a little apprehensive when I motioned Mary Huston, the town historian, into the staff area of the library. This was it: his first introduction to the public. As I took the kitten in my arms, I must admit that I felt a flutter in *my* heart. When the kitten had looked into my eyes, something had happened; we had made a connection. He was more than just a cat to me. It had only been a day, but already I couldn't stand the thought of being without him. What if Mary didn't like him?

"Why hello," Mary said with a smile when she saw the tiny kitten in my hands. She reached out to pet him on the top of the head—and he stretched out to sniff her hand!

"Oh, my," Mary said. "He's handsome."

Handsome. There was no other way to describe him. This was a handsome cat. His coat was a mix of vibrant orange and white with subtle darker stripes. It grew longer as he got older, but as a kitten it was thick and long only around his neck. A lot of cats have pointy noses, or their mouths jut out a bit too far, or they're a little lop-sided, but this kitten's face was perfect. And his eyes, those huge golden eyes!

But it wasn't just his looks that made him beautiful; it was also his personality. If you cared at all about cats, you just had to hold him. There was something in his face—in the way he looked at you—that called out for love.

"He likes to be cradled," I said, gently sliding him into Mary's arms. "On his back. Like a baby."

"A one-pound baby."

"I don't think he even weighs that much."

The kitten shook his tail and nestled down into Mary's arms.

"Oh, Vicki," Mary said. "He's adorable. What's his name?"

A good question, since he didn't actually have a name. I'd started calling him Dewey, but that was only because I had to call him something. Since he wasn't my cat, I didn't have the right to name him. The patrons of the library would get to do that . . . if they wanted us to keep him.

"We're calling him Dewey," I told Mary, "but that's just a nickname for now."

"Hi, Dewey," Mary said. "Do you like the library?"

Dewey stared into Mary's face, then nuzzled her arm with his head.

Mary looked up with a smile. "I could hold him all day."

But, of course, she didn't. She put Dewey back into my arms, and I took him around the corner. The entire staff was waiting for us.

"That went well," I said. "One person down, 9,999 people to go."

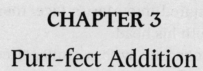

CHAPTER 3

Purr-fect Addition

Slowly, we started introducing Dewey to more regular visitors who loved cats. He was still weak, so we passed him directly into their arms. Marcie Muckey was instantly smitten. Mike Baehr and his wife, Peg, loved him. Pat Jones and Judy Johnson thought he was adorable. Actually there were four Judy Johnsons among the ten thousand people in Spencer. Two were regular library users, and both were Dewey fans.

A week later, Dewey's story ran on the front page of the *Spencer Daily Reporter* under the headline "Purr-fect Addition Made to Spencer Library." The article, which took up half the page, told the story of Dewey's miraculous rescue and was accompanied by a color photograph of a tiny orange kitten staring shyly but confidently into the camera from atop an old-fashioned pull-drawer card catalog.

For a week, Dewey had been a secret. If you didn't come into the library, you didn't know about him. Now everyone in town knew. Many people, especially children, loved the idea of having a cat in the library. Most people didn't give Dewey a second thought.

But there were some complainers. I was a little disappointed, I must admit, but not surprised. There is nothing on earth that someone won't complain about.

One woman took particular offense. She sent me a letter that was pure fire and brimstone. According to her, I was a madwoman who was not only threatening the health of every innocent child in town, but also destroying the values of the community. An animal! In a library! If we let that stand, what was to stop people from walking a cow down Grand Avenue? In fact, she threatened to show up in the library that very afternoon with her cow on a leash.

But you know what? I looked up her name in our files. She'd never checked a book out from the library. Never. In fact, she didn't even have a library card!

But I did get some worried phone calls. "My child has allergies," one woman said. "What am I going to do? He loves the library."

I knew allergies would be the most common concern, so I was prepared. A year earlier, Muffin, the beloved cat-in-residence at the Putnam Valley Library in upstate New York, had been banished after a library board member developed a severe cat allergy. As a consequence, the library lost $80,000 in promised donations. I had no intention of letting my cat, or my library, go the way of Muffin.

Spencer was too small for an allergist, so I asked the advice of two general practice doctors. The Spencer Public Library, they noted, was a large, open space sectioned off by rows of four-foot-high shelves. The staff area was enclosed by a temporary wall, leaving six feet open to the ceiling. There were two door-size openings in that wall, and since neither had a door, they were always open. Even the staff area was an open space, with desks pushed back-to-back or separated by bookshelves.

Not only did this layout allow Dewey easy

access to the safety of the staff area, but the doctors assured me it would also prevent the buildup of dander and hair. The library, apparently, was perfectly designed to prevent allergies. If anyone on staff had been allergic it might have been a problem, but a few hours of exposure every couple of days? The doctors agreed there was nothing to worry about.

The parents were skeptical, but most brought their children to the library for a trial run. I held Dewey in my arms for each visit. I didn't know how the parents would react or how Dewey would respond because the children were so excited to see him. Their mothers and fathers would tell them to be gentle. The children would approach slowly and whisper, "Hi, Dewey," and then explode with squeals as their parents ushered them away with a quick, "That's enough." Dewey didn't mind the noise; he was the calmest kitten I'd ever seen. He did mind, I think, that these children weren't allowed to pet him.

But a few days later, one family came back with a camera. And this time the allergic little boy was sitting beside Dewey, petting him, while his mother took pictures.

"Justin can't have pets," she told me. "I never

knew how much he missed them. He loves Dewey already."

I loved Dewey already, too. We all loved Dewey. How could you resist his charm? He was affectionate, social, beautiful—and still limping on his tiny frostbitten feet.

What I couldn't believe was how much Dewey loved us. How comfortable he seemed around strangers. His attitude seemed to be *How can anyone resist me?* I soon realized that Dewey didn't think of himself as just another cat.

He always thought of himself, correctly, as one of a kind.

CHAPTER 4

Dewey Readmore Books

Dewey was a lucky cat. He not only survived the freezing library drop box, but also fell into the arms of a staff that loved him and a library perfectly designed to care for him. There were no two ways about it, Dewey led a charmed life. But Spencer was also lucky, because Dewey couldn't have fallen into our lives at a better time. That winter wasn't just cold; it was one of the worst times in Spencer's history.

Spencer was a farming town. For miles around, all you could see were farms. But in the 1980s, there was a farm crisis. Land was too expensive, crop prices were too cheap, and farms started to go out of business. When the farmers couldn't pay their loans, the banks failed. Then the stores closed because there was nobody to buy their goods. People lost their jobs. More farms closed. After a while, it felt like the whole region was being pulled steadily down. There was even a running joke: The last store owner out of downtown Spencer, please turn off the lights.

Then into our lives came Dewey. I don't want to make too much of that, because Dewey didn't put food on anyone's table. He didn't create jobs. He didn't turn our economy around. Dewey was a welcome distraction.

But he was so much more, too. Dewey's story resonated with the people of Spencer. Here was an alley cat, left for dead in a freezing drop box, terrified, alone, and clinging to life. He made it through that dark night, and that terrible event turned out to be the best thing that ever happened to him. He never lost his trust, no matter what the circumstances, or his appreciation for life. From the moment we found him, Dewey believed everything was going to be fine.

And when he was around, he made others believe that, too. It took him ten days to get healthy enough to explore the library on his own, and once he did, it was clear he had no interest in books and shelves. His interest was people. If there was a patron in the library, he'd walk straight up to her—still slow on his sore feet—and jump into her lap. Often he was pushed away, but rejection never deterred him. Dewey kept jumping, kept looking for laps to lie in and hands to pet him, and things started to change.

I noticed it first with the older patrons, who often came to the library to flip through magazines or browse for books. Once Dewey started spending time with them, they showed up more frequently and stayed longer. The ones who had always given the staff a friendly wave or good morning now engaged us in conversation, and that conversation was usually about Dewey. They couldn't get enough Dewey stories. They weren't just filling their time now; they were visiting friends.

One older man in particular came in at the same time every morning, sat in the same big, comfortable chair, and read the newspaper. His wife had recently passed away, and he was lonely. I didn't expect him to be a cat person, but from the first moment Dewey climbed into his lap, the man was beaming. Suddenly he wasn't reading the newspaper alone anymore.

"Are you happy here, Dewey?" the man would ask every morning as he petted his new friend. Dewey would shut his eyes and, more often than not, drop off to sleep.

And then there was the man looking for a job. I didn't know him, but I knew his type—proud, hardworking, probably a father with kids at home—and I knew he was suffering. He was from Spencer, a laborer, not a farmer. His job-hunting outfit, like his former work outfit, was jeans and a regular shirt. Every morning, Dewey approached him, and every morning the man pushed him away. Then one day I saw Dewey sitting on his lap, and for the first time in weeks, the man was smiling. There was still sadness in his eyes, but he was smiling.

Maybe Dewey couldn't give much, but in the winter of 1988 he gave exactly what Spencer needed. So I gave our kitten to the town. The staff understood. He wasn't our cat. He belonged to the patrons of the Spencer Public Library. I put a box by the front door and told people, "You know the cat who sits on your lap? The one who reads the newspaper with you? Who steals the lipstick out of your purse and knocks your pencils to the ground? Well, he's your cat, and I want you to help name him."

I had been library director for only six months, so I was still enthusiastic about contests. Every few weeks we put a box in the lobby, made an announcement on the local radio station, and offered a prize for the winning entry. A good contest with a good prize might draw fifty entries. If the prize was expensive, like a television set, we might scrape up seventy. Usually we got about twenty-five.

Our Name the Kitty contest, which wasn't mentioned on the radio because I wanted only regular patrons to participate, and didn't even offer a prize, received 397 entries. Three hundred ninety-seven entries! That's when I realized the library had stumbled onto something important. Community interest in Dewey was off all our charts!

Lasagna-loving Garfield was at the height of his popularity, so Garfield was a popular name choice. There were nine votes for Tiger. Tigger was almost as popular. Morris was another multiple vote-getter. Even cultural blips like ALF (a cuddly alien puppet with his own television show) and Spuds (after Spuds MacKenzie, a dog in television commercials) received votes. There were a few mean-spirited entries, like Fleabag, and some that were just plain weird, like Cat-gang Amadeus Taffy (a sudden sweet tooth?), Ladybooks (an odd name for a boy), Hop-snopper, Boxcar, and Nukster.

By far the most entries, more than fifty, were for Dewey. Apparently the patrons had already grown attached to this kitten, and they didn't want him to change. Not even his name. And to be honest, the staff didn't, either. We, too, had grown attached to Dewey just the way he was.

Still, the name needed something. So we decided to think of a last name. Mary Walk, our children's librarian, suggested Readmore. A commercial running during the Saturday morning cartoons—this was back when cartoons were only shown before noon on Saturdays, if you can believe it—featured a cartoon cat named O. G. Readmore who encouraged kids to "read a book and take a look at the TV in your head." I'm sure that's where the name came from.

Dewey Readmore. Hmmm. Close, but not quite. I suggested the last name Books.

Dewey Readmore Books. One name for the

librarians, who live by the Dewey decimal system. One for the children, who loved cartoons. One for the written word.

Do We Read More Books? A challenge to be well-read. A name to put us in the mood to learn.

Dewey Readmore Books. Three names for our regal, confident, beautiful cat. I'm sure we'd have named him Sir Dewey Readmore Books if we had thought of it, but we were librarians; we didn't stand on pomp and circumstance. And neither did Dewey. He always went by his first name or, occasionally, just "the Dew."

CHAPTER 5

The Dewey Carry

C ats are creatures of habit, and it didn't take long for Dewey to develop a routine. When I arrived at the library every morning, he was waiting for me at the front door. He would take a few bites of his food while I hung up my jacket and bag, and then we would walk the library together, making sure everything was in place and discussing our evenings. Dewey was more a sniffer than a talker, but I didn't mind.

After our walk, Dewey would visit the staff. If someone was having a bad morning, he'd spend extra time with her. He had an amazing sense of who needed him, and he was always willing to give his time. But never for too long. At two minutes to nine, Dewey would drop whatever he was doing and race for the front door.

A patron was always waiting outside at exactly nine o'clock when we opened the doors, and she would usually enter with a warm, "Hi, Dewey. How are you this morning?"

Welcome, welcome, I imagined him saying from his post to the left of the door. *Why don't you pet the cat?*

No response. The early birds were usually there for a reason, which meant they didn't have time to stop for a cat.

No petting? Fine. There's always another person where you came from—wherever that is.

It wouldn't take long for him to find a lap, and since he'd been up for two hours that usually meant it was time for a nap. Dewey was already so comfortable in the library he had no problem falling asleep in public places. He could fall asleep anywhere.

Dewey preferred laps for naps, but if they weren't available he would curl up in a box. The cards for the catalog came in small boxes about the size of a pair of baby shoes. Dewey liked to cram all four feet inside, sit down, and let his sides ooze over the edge. If he found a bigger box, he buried his head and tail in the bottom. The only thing you could see was a big blob of back fur sticking out of the top. He looked like a muffin.

Once, I watched him slowly wind his way into a half-empty tissue box. He put his two front feet through the slit on top, then delicately stepped in with the other two. Slowly he sat down on his hind legs and rolled his back end until it was wedged into the box. Then he started bending his front legs and working the front of his body into the crease. The operation took four or five minutes, but finally there was nothing left but his head sticking out in one direction and his tail sticking out in the other. He just stared into the distance, pretending the rest of the world didn't exist.

In those days, Iowa provided envelopes with its tax forms, and we always put a box of them out for patrons. Dewey must have spent half his first winter curled up in that box.

"I need an envelope," a patron would say nervously, "but I don't want to disturb Dewey. What should I do?"

"Don't worry. He's asleep."

"But won't it wake him up? He's lying on top of them."

"Oh, no, the Dew's dead to the world."

The patron would gently roll Dewey to the side and then, far more carefully than necessary, slide out an envelope. He could have jerked it like a magician pulling a tablecloth from under a dinner setting, it wouldn't have mattered. Dewey was an expert when it came to napping.

"Cat hair comes with the envelope," I'd say. "No charge."

Dewey's other favorite resting spot was the back of the copier.

"Don't worry," I told the confused patrons, "you can't disturb him. He sleeps there because it's warm. The more copies you make, the more heat the machine produces, and the happier he'll be."

The staff, meanwhile, had no such hesitation when it came to the Dew. One of my first decisions was that no library funds, not one penny, would ever be spent on Dewey's care. Instead, we kept a Dewey Box in the back room. Everyone on staff tossed in their loose change. Most of us also brought in soda cans. Cynthia Behrends would take the cans to a recycling drop-off every week and exchange them for a few dollars. The whole staff was feeding our kitty.

In return for these small contributions, we'd get endless hours of pleasure. Dewey loved drawers, and he developed a habit of popping out of them and scaring the pants off us. If you were shelving books, he'd jump onto the cart and demand a trip around the library. And when Kim Peterson, the library secretary, started typing, you knew a show was about to begin. As soon as I heard those keys, I'd put down my work and wait for the signal.

"Dewey's after the clacker thingies again!" Kim would call out.

I'd hurry out of my office to find Dewey hunched on the back of Kim's big white typewriter. His head would be jerking from side to side as the disk moved left to right, then back again, until finally he couldn't take it anymore and lunged at the "clacker thingies," which were the keys rising up to strike the paper. The whole staff would be there, watching and laughing. Dewey's antics always drew a crowd.

But no matter how much fun Dewey was having, he never forgot his routine. At exactly ten thirty, he would hop up and head for the staff room. Jean ate yogurt on her break, and if he hung around long enough, she'd let him lick the lid. Jean was quiet and hardworking, but she always found ways to accommodate Dewey. If Dewey wanted downtime, he would lie limply over Jean's left shoulder—and only her left shoulder, never her right.

After a few months, when Dewey wouldn't let us hold him cradled in our arms anymore (too much like a baby, I guess), the whole staff adopted Jean's over-the-shoulder technique. We called it the Dewey Carry.

CHAPTER 6

Dewey's Least Favorite Things

Dewey helped me with downtime, too, which was nice, since I had a tendency to work too hard. Many days I'd be hunched over my desk for hours, so intent on my work that I wouldn't even realize Dewey was there until he sprang into my lap.

"How you doing, baby boy?" I'd say with a smile. "So nice to see you."

I'd pet him a few times before turning back to my work. Unsatisfied, he'd climb on my desk and start sniffing.

"Oh, you just happened, *accidentally*, to sit on the paper I'm working on, didn't you?"

I'd put him on the floor. He'd hop back up.

"Not now, Dewey. I'm busy." I'd put him back down.

He'd hop back up.

Maybe if I ignore him, I'd think, *he'll lose interest.*

Nope. Dewey would push his head against my pencil.

I'd push him aside.

Fine, he'd think, *I'll knock these pens to the ground.* Which he proceeded to do, one pen at a time. I couldn't help but laugh.

"Okay, Dewey, you win." I'd wad up a piece of paper and throw it to him. He'd run after it, sniff it, then come back. Typical cat.

I'd walk over, pick up the paper, and toss it a few more times.

"What am I going to do with you?"

But it wasn't all jokes and games. I was the boss, and I had responsibilities—like giving the cat a bath. The first time I bathed Dewey, I was confident things would go well. He loved the bath that first morning, right?

This time, Dewey slid calmly into the sink... and completely freaked out as soon as he touched the water. He thrashed. He screamed. He put his feet on the edge of the sink and tried to throw his body over the side. What did he think, all that water was going to melt him? Twenty minutes later, both of us were soaking wet and exhausted. Dewey's fur was twisted up in knots. My hair looked like I had stuck my tongue in a light socket. Everybody laughed.

The next bath was just as bad. I managed to get Dewey scrubbed, but I didn't have the patience for toweling and blow-drying. Not this crazy kitten.

"Fine," I told him. "If you hate it that much, just go."

Dewey was a vain cat. He would spend an hour washing his face. The funniest part was the way he would ball up his fist, lick it, and shove it into his ears. He would work those ears until they were sparkling white. Now, soaking wet, he looked like a some sort of hairy sea creature that had washed up on the beach. It was pathetic. The staff was laughing and taking pictures, but Dewey looked so genuinely upset that after a few minutes the pictures stopped.

"Have a sense of humor, Dew," I teased him. "You brought this on yourself."

He curled up behind a shelf of books and didn't come out for hours. After that, Dewey and I agreed that two baths a year were plenty.

"If you thought the bath was bad," I told Dewey a few months into his stay at the library, "you're not going to like this at all." I wrapped him in his green towel and brought him to the car.

Five minutes later, we arrived at Dr. Esterly's office. There were several veterinarians in Spencer—after all, we lived in an area prone to breech-birth cows, distressed hogs, and sick farm dogs—but I preferred Dr. Esterly. He was a quiet, modest man with an extremely deliberate way of speaking. His voice was deep and slow like a lazy river, and he didn't rush. He was a big man but his hands were gentle. And he loved animals.

"Hi, Dewey," he said, checking him over.

I looked down at Dewey's tiny paws, which had finally healed. There were tufts of fur sticking out from between his toes. "Do you think he's part Persian?"

Dr. Esterley looked at Dewey. His regal bearing. The glorious ruff of long orange fur around his neck.

"No. He's just a good-looking alley cat."

I didn't believe it for a second.

He was a lion in alley cat clothing.

"Dewey is a product of survival of the fittest,"

Dr. Esterly continued. "His ancestors have probably lived in that alley for generations."

"So he's one of us."

Dr. Esterly smiled. "I suppose so. You'll just need to leave him with me overnight."

"Do you think this is absolutely necessary, Doctor?"

"Cats need to be neutered," he said as he picked Dewey up and held him under his arm.

Dewey was relaxed and purring. The last thing Dr. Esterly said before they disappeared around the corner was, "Dewey is one fine cat."

He sure was. And I missed him already.

When I picked Dewey up the next morning, my heart almost broke in two. He had a faraway look in his eyes, and a little shaved belly. I took him in my arms. He pushed his head against me and started purring. He was so happy to see his old pal Vicki.

Back at the library, the staff dropped everything. "Poor baby. Poor baby," they said. I gave him over to their care—Dewey was with friends, after all—and went back to work. One more set of hands and he might be crushed. Besides, the trip to the vet's office had put me behind, and I had a mountain of work.

But I wasn't alone for long. An hour later, as I was hanging up the phone, I looked up to see Dewey hobbling through my office door. I knew he'd been getting love and attention from the rest of the staff, but I could tell from his determined wobbling that he needed something more.

Sure, cats can be fun, but my relationship with Dewey was already far more. He was so intelligent. He was so playful. He treated people so well. I didn't yet have as deep a bond with him as I would later, but already I loved him.

And he loved me back. Not like he loved everyone else, but in a special and deeper way. The look he gave me that first morning meant something. It really did. Never was that more clear than now, as he pushed toward me with such determination. I could almost hear him saying, *Where have you been? I missed you.*

I reached down, scooped him up, and cradled him against my chest. I don't know if I said it out loud or to myself, but it didn't matter. Dewey could already read my moods. "I'm your mama, aren't I?"

Dewey put his head on my shoulder, right up against my neck, and purred.

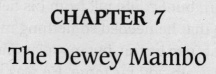

CHAPTER 7

The Dewey Mambo

Don't get me wrong, everything wasn't perfect with the Dew. Yes, he was a sweet and beautiful cat, and yes, he was extraordinarily trusting and generous, but he was still a kitten. He'd streak crazily through the staff room. He'd knock your work to the floor out of pure playfulness. Sometimes he wouldn't take no for an answer when a patron wanted to be left alone. At Story Hour, his presence would make the children so rambunctious that Mary Walk, our children's librarian, banned him from the room.

Then there was Mark, a large fabric puppet of a child with muscular dystrophy that we used to teach schoolchildren about disabilities. Every night, Dewey would sleep on the puppet. There was so much cat hair on Mark's legs that we finally had to put him in a closet. Dewey worked all night until he figured out how to open that closet, then he went right back to sleeping on Mark's lap. We bought a lock for the closet the next day.

But nothing compared to his behavior around catnip. Doris Armstrong was always bringing Dewey presents, such as little balls or toy mice. Doris had cats of her own, and she always thought of Dewey when she went to the pet store for their litter and food. One day near the end of Dewey's first summer, she quite innocently brought in a bag of fresh catnip. Dewey was so excited by the smell I thought he was going to climb her leg. For the first time in his life, the cat actually begged.

When Doris finally crumbled a few leaves on the floor, Dewey went crazy. He started smelling them so hard I thought he was going to inhale the floor. After a few sniffs, he started sneezing, but he didn't slow down. Instead, he started chewing the leaves, then alternating back and forth: chewing, sniffing, chewing, sniffing.

His muscles started to ripple, a slow cascade of tension flowing out of his bones and down his back.

When he finally shook that tension out the end of his tail, he flopped over on the ground and rolled back and forth in the catnip. He rolled until he lost every bone in his body. Unable to walk, he slithered on the floor, undulating as he rubbed his chin along the carpet like a snowplow blade. I mean, the cat oozed.

Then, gradually, Dewey's spine bent backward, in slow motion, until his head was resting on his behind. Cat-bent-in-half. But he didn't stop there. He formed figure eights, zigzags, pretzels. I swear the front half of his body wasn't even connected to the back half. We called it the Dewey Mambo.

When he accidentally ended up flat on his tummy, he rippled his way back to the catnip and started rolling in it all over again. Eventually, Dewey rolled over onto his back, lifted his back legs, and started kicking himself in the chin. The kicks started out fast, but they got slower and slower and slower until, finally, with a few weak kicks hanging feebly in the air, Dewey fell asleep right on top of the last of the catnip. My goodness, it was funny!

Dewey never tired of catnip. And every time he got hold of some, it was the same thing: the Dewey Mambo, the chin kicks, and then, finally, one very tired cat fast asleep on the library floor.

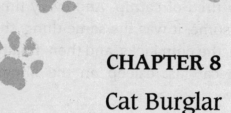

CHAPTER 8
Cat Burglar

Dewey's other major interest—besides people, puppets, drawers, boxes, copiers, typewriters, and catnip—was rubber bands. Dewey was absolutely fanatical about rubber bands. He didn't even need to see them; he could smell them across the library. As soon as you put a box of rubber bands on your desk, he was there.

"Here you go, Dewey," I would say as I opened a new bag. "One for you and one for me." He would take his rubber band in his mouth and happily skip away.

I would find it the next morning...you know, in his...litter box. It looked like a worm poking its head out of a chunk of dirt. I thought, *That can't be good.*

I decided to address this at our staff meeting. Dewey always attended the meetings, but fortunately he wasn't able to understand what we were talking about. So I ended the meeting with a gentle reminder: "Don't give Dewey any more rubber bands. I don't care how much he begs. He's been eating them, and I have a feeling rubber isn't the healthiest food for a growing kitten."

The next day, there were more rubber band worms in Dewey's litter. And the next. And the next.

At the next staff meeting, I was more direct. "Is anyone giving Dewey rubber bands?"

No. No. No. No. No.

"Then he must be stealing them. From now on, don't leave rubber bands lying out on your desk."

Easier said than done. Much, much easier said than done. You would be amazed how many rubber bands there are in a library. We all put our rubber band holders away, but that didn't even dent the problem. Rubber bands are sneaky critters. They slide under computer keyboards and crawl into your pencil holder. They fall under your desk and hide in the wires. One evening I even caught Dewey rummaging through a stack of work on someone's desk. There was a rubber band lurking every time he pushed a piece of paper aside.

"Even the hidden ones need to go," I said at the next staff meeting. "Let's clean up those desks and put them away. Remember, Dewey can *smell* rubber." In just a few days, the staff area looked neater than it had in years.

So Dewey started raiding the rubber bands left on the circulation desk for patrons. We stashed them in a drawer. He found the rubber bands by the copier, too. Those went into another drawer. The patrons were just going to have to ask for rubber bands. A small price to pay, I thought, for a cat that spent most of his day trying to make them happy.

Soon, our rubber band operation was showing signs of success. There were still rubber worms in the litter box but not nearly as many. And Dewey was being forced into brazenness. Every time I pulled out a rubber band, he was watching me.

"Getting desperate, are we?"

As soon as I put the rubber band down, Dewey pounced. I pushed him away; he sat on the desk waiting for his chance. "Not this time, Dewey," I said with a grin. I admit, this game was fun.

Dewey became more subtle. He waited for you to turn your back, then pounced on the rubber band left innocently lying on your desk. It had been there five minutes. Humans forget. Not cats. Dewey remembered every drawer left open a crack, then came back that night to wiggle his way inside. He never messed up the contents of the drawer. The next morning, the rubber bands were simply gone.

One afternoon I was walking past our big floor-to-ceiling supply cabinet. I was focused on something else, and only noticed the open door out of the corner of my eye. "Did I just see..."

I turned around and walked back to the cabinet. Sure enough, there was Dewey, sitting on a shelf, a huge rubber band hanging out of his mouth.

You can't stop the Dew! I'm going to be feasting for a week.

I had to laugh. In general, Dewey was the best-behaved kitten I had ever seen. He never knocked books or displays off shelves. If I told him not to do something, he usually stopped. He was unfailingly kind to strangers and staffers alike. For a kitten, he was downright mellow. But he was absolutely incorrigible when it came to rubber bands. The cat would go anywhere and do anything to sink his teeth into a rubber band.

"Hold on, Dewey," I told him, putting down my pile of work. "I'm going to get a picture of this." By the time I got back with the camera, the cat and his rubber band were gone.

"Make sure all the cabinets and drawers are completely closed," I reminded the staff. Dewey was already notorious. He had a habit of getting closed inside cabinets and then leaping out at the next person to open them. We weren't sure if it was a game or an accident, but Dewey clearly enjoyed it.

A few mornings later I found file cards sitting unbound on the front desk. Dewey had never gone for tight rubber bands before; now, he started biting them off every night. As always, he was delicate even in defiance. He left perfectly neat stacks, not a card out of place. The cards went into the drawers; the drawers were shut tight.

After nine months, you could spend an entire day in the Spencer Public Library without seeing a rubber band. Oh, they were still there, but they were hidden away where only those with opposable thumbs could get to them. It was the ultimate cleaning operation. The library looked beautiful; we were proud. There was just one problem: Dewey was still chewing rubber bands.

I put together an investigative team. It took us two days to find Dewey's last good source: the coffee mug on Mary Walk's desk.

"Mary," I said, flipping a notebook like the police detective in a bad television drama, "we have reason to believe the rubber bands are coming from your mug."

"That's impossible. I've never seen Dewey around my desk."

"Evidence suggests the suspect is intentionally avoiding your desk to throw us off the trail. We believe he only approaches the mug at night."

"What evidence?"

I pointed to several small pieces of chewed rubber band on the floor. "He chews them up and spits them out. He eats them for breakfast. I think you know all the usual clichés."

Mary shuddered at the thought of the garbage on the floor having passed into and out of the stomach of a cat. Still, it seemed so improbable...

"The mug is six inches deep. It's full of paper clips, staples, pens, pencils. How could he possibly pluck out rubber bands without knocking everything over?"

"Where there's a will, there's a way. And this suspect has proven, in all his months at the library, that he has the will."

"But there are hardly any rubber bands in there! Surely this isn't his only source!"

"How about an experiment? You put the mug in the cabinet, we'll see if he pukes rubber bands in the morning."

"But this mug has my children's pictures on it!"

"Good point. How about we just remove the rubber bands?"

Mary decided to put a lid on the mug. The next morning, the lid was on her desk with teeth marks along one edge. No doubt about it, the mug was the source. The rubber bands went into a drawer. Convenience was sacrificed for the greater good.

We never completely succeeded in wiping out Dewey's rubber band fixation—or his supply. He'd lose interest, only to go back on the prowl a few months or even a few years later. In the end, it was more a game than a battle, a contest of wits versus will. We had the wits; Dewey had the will. And he had that powerful, rubber-sniffing nose.

CHAPTER 9

Best Friends

Now let's not make too much of this. Rubber bands were a hobby, that's all. Catnip and boxes were mere distractions. Dewey's true love was people, and there was nothing he wouldn't do for his adoring public.

I remember standing at the circulation desk one morning talking with Doris when we noticed a toddler wobbling by. She must have learned to walk recently, because her balance was shaky and her steps uneven. It wasn't helping that her arms were wrapped tightly across her chest, clutching Dewey in a bear hug. His rear and tail were sticking up in her face, and his head was hanging down toward the floor. Doris and

I stopped talking and watched in amazement as the little girl toddled in slow motion across the library, a very big smile on her face and a very resigned cat hanging upside down from her arms.

"Amazing," Doris said.

"I should do something about that," I said. But I didn't. I knew Dewey was in control of the situation. No matter what happened, he could take care of himself.

And besides, he had the whole library wrapped around his paw. When regular patrons came in and Dewey wasn't there to greet them, they'd go looking for him. That's the subtle difference between a cat and a dog, my friends: A dog finds you; a cat waits for you to find them.

First patrons searched the floor, figuring Dewey was hiding around a corner. Then they checked the top of the bookshelves. "Oh, how are you, Dewey? I didn't see you there," they would say, reaching up to pet him.

Dewey would give them the top of his head to pet, that's all. But as soon as they forgot about him, Dewey jumped into their laps. That's when I saw the smiles. By the end of his first year, dozens of patrons were telling me, "I know Dewey likes everyone, but I have a special relationship with him."

I smiled and nodded. *That's right, Judy,* I thought. *You and everyone else who comes into this library.*

Dewey's real favorites, though, were the children. If you wanted to understand the effect Dewey had on Spencer, all you had to do was look at the children. The smiles when they came into the library, the joy as they searched and called for him, the excitement when they found him.

The children wanted his attention, a fact that became very noticeable during Story Hour. Every Tuesday morning, the murmur of excited children in the Round Room, where Story Hour was held, would be suddenly punctuated by a cry of "Dewey's here!" A mad rush would ensue as every child in the room tried to pet Dewey at the same time.

"If you don't settle down," our children's librarian, Mary Walk, would tell them, "Dewey has to go."

A barely contained hush would fall over the room as the children took their seats, trying their best to contain their excitement. When they were relatively calm, Dewey would begin sliding between them, rubbing against each child and making them all giggle. Soon kids were grabbing at him and whispering, "Sit with me, Dewey. Sit with me."

"Children, don't make me warn you again."

"Yes, Mary." The children always called the librarians by their first names.

Dewey, knowing he had pushed the limit, would stop wandering and curl up in the lap of one lucky child. He didn't let a child grab him and hold him; he *chose* someone. And every week it was a different child.

Once he had chosen a lap, Dewey usually sat quietly for the whole hour. Unless a movie was being shown. Then he would jump on a table, curl his legs under his body, and watch the screen intently. When the credits rolled he'd feign boredom and jump down. Before the children could ask "Where's Dewey?", he was gone.

Dewey also won over the older kids. Spencer Middle School was across the street from the library, and about fifty students stayed with us after school while their parents were working. On the days they blew in like a hurricane, Dewey avoided them, especially the rowdy ones who pretended to be too cool for things like cats. But on calmer days he would mingle.

He had many friends among the students, both boys and girls. They petted him and played games with him, like rolling pencils off the table and watching his surprise when they disappeared. One girl would wiggle a pen out the end of her coat sleeve. Dewey would chase the pen up into the sleeve and then, deciding he liked that warm, dark, tight place, he'd sometimes lie down for a nap. Only his head would be sticking out, sort of like a hot dog peeking out from the end of a bun.

There was one child, though, Dewey couldn't win over. She was four years old when Dewey arrived, and she came to the library every week with her mother and older brother. Her brother loved Dewey, but she hung back as far as possible, looking tense and nervous. Her mother eventually confided in me that the girl was afraid of all four-legged animals, especially cats and dogs.

What an opportunity! I knew Dewey could do for this girl what he had done for the children with cat allergies who finally had a cat to spend time with. I suggested exposing her gently to

Dewey, first by looking through the window at him and then with supervised meetings.

"This is an ideal job for our gentle, loving Dewey," I told her mother. I was so enthusiastic, I even researched the best books to help the girl overcome her fear.

Her mother didn't want to go that route, so instead of trying to change the girl's feelings about cats, I accommodated her. When the girl came to the door and waved at the clerk at the front desk, we found Dewey and locked him in my office. Dewey hated being locked in my office, especially when patrons were in the library. *You don't have to do this,* I could hear him howling. *I know who she is! I won't go near her!*

I hated to lock him away, and I hated to miss the opportunity for Dewey to make this little girl's life better, but what could I do? *Don't force it, Vicki,* I told myself. *It will come.*

With that in mind I planned a low-key celebration for Dewey's first birthday: just a cake made out of cat food for Dewey, and a normal one for the patrons. We didn't know exactly when he was born, but Dr. Esterly had estimated he was eight weeks old when we found him, so we counted back to late November and chose the

55

eighteenth. We had found Dewey on January 18, so we figured that was his lucky day.

A week before the celebration, we put out a card for signatures. Within days there were more than a hundred. At the next Story Hour, the children colored pictures of birthday cakes. Four days before the party, we strung the pictures on a clothesline behind the circulation desk. Then the newspaper ran a story, and we started receiving birthday cards in the mail. I couldn't believe it—people were sending birthday cards to a cat!

By the time the party rolled around, the kids were jumping up and down with excitement. Another cat would have been frightened, no doubt, but Dewey took it all in with his usual calm. Instead of interacting with the kids, though, he kept his eyes on the prize: his cat-food cake in the shape of a mouse, covered with Jean Hollis Clark's brand of full-fat yogurt (Dewey hated the diet stuff). As the kids smiled and giggled, I looked out at the parents gathered at the back of the crowd. They were smiling as much as the children.

DEWEY'S LIKES AND DISLIKES

(WRITTEN ON A BIG ORANGE POSTER BOARD FOR DEWEY'S FIRST BIRTHDAY ON NOVEMBER 18)

CATEGORY	♥ ♥ LOVES ♥ ♥	✖ ✖ HATES ✖ ✖
FOOD	Purina Special Dinners, Dairy Flavor	Anything else!
PLACE TO SLEEP	Any box or lap	Alone or in his own basket
TOY	Anything with catnip	Toys that don't move
TIME OF DAY	8:00 a.m. when the staff arrives	When everybody leaves
BODY POSITION	Stretched out on his back	Standing up for very long
TEMPERATURE	Warm, warm, warm	Cold, cold, cold
HIDING PLACE	Between the Westerns on the bottom shelf	The lobby
ACTIVITY	Making new friends, watching the copier	Going to the vet
PETTING	On the head, behind his ears	Scratched or touched on his stomach
EQUIPMENT	Kim's typewriter, the copier	Vacuum cleaner
ANIMAL	Himself!	None
GROOMING	Cleaning his ears	Being brushed or combed
MEDICINE	Felaxin (for hair balls)	Anything else
GAME	Hide-and-seek, pushing pen on the floor	Wrestling
PEOPLE	Almost everyone	People who are mean to him
NOISE	A snack being opened, paper rustling	Loud trucks, construction, dogs barking
BOOK	*The Cat Who Would Be King*	*101 Uses for a Dead Cat*

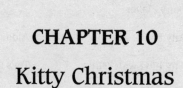

CHAPTER 10

Kitty Christmas

S hortly after Dewey's birthday, it was time for what would become his favorite holiday: Christmas. Now Christmas, you have to understand, was a holiday the town of Spencer celebrated together. The season started on the first weekend in December with the Grand Meander, a walking tour of Grand Avenue.

The street was strung with white lights; Christmas music was piped in; Santa Claus came to receive wish lists from the children (yes, even in the bad years he made it). The whole town was out, laughing, talking, and clutching one another to share the warmth. The stores stayed open late, showing off their holiday selections and offering cookies and hot chocolate to fight off the biting cold.

Every storefront window was decorated. We called them Living Windows, because in each one local residents acted out holiday scenes. The Parker Museum always created a vision of a pioneer Christmas. Other windows showcased the 1950s (my childhood!), with Radio Flyers and hula hoops. Some had mangers. Others featured toy tractors and cars for a boy's view of Christmas morning, or porcelain dolls for a girl's.

On the corner of First Avenue and Fifth Street, at the end of the Great Meander walk, the Festival of Trees, a Christmas tree decorating contest, was held. Since this was Dewey's first Christmas in Spencer, the library had entered a tree under the title "Do-We Love Christmas?" The tree was decorated with—what else?—pictures of Dewey. It also featured puffy kitten ornaments and garlands of red yarn. The presents under the tree were books like *The Cat-a-log* and *The Cat in the Hat*, tied in neat red bows. There was no official judging, but I think "Do-We Love Christmas?" was the winning Christmas tree that year, hands down.

But for Dewey, the real celebration began the next day in the library.

Every year, on the Monday after the Grand Meander, I took the Christmas decorations down from the top shelves of the library storage room. Cynthia Behrends and I always arrived early to set up and decorate the most important part: our big artificial Christmas tree. Cynthia was the hardest worker on staff and eagerly volunteered for every job. But she didn't know what she was getting into because this year, when we slid the long thin Christmas tree box off its high shelf, we had company.

"Dewey's excited this morning," she said. "He must like the looks of this box."

"Or the smell of all those plastic branches."

I could see his nose sniffing ninety odors a minute and his mind racing. *Could it be? Could it really be? All this time, could Mom have been hiding the world's largest, most spectacular, most deliciously smelly rubber band?*

When we started pulling the Christmas tree out of the box, I could almost see Dewey's jaw drop. *It's not a rubber band, it's...it's...better.*

As we pulled out each branch, Dewey lunged at it. He wanted to sniff and chew and steal every green piece of plastic sticking out of every green wire branch.

"Give me that, Dewey!" I yelled.

He coughed a few plastic tree needles onto the floor. Then he leaped into the box just as Cynthia was pulling out the next branch.

"Back off, Dewey."

Cynthia pulled him out, but a second later he was back, a green needle stuck to the moist tip of his nose. This time, his whole head disappeared inside the box.

"This isn't going to work, Dewey. Do you want me to get the rest of the tree out or not?"

Apparently the answer was not, because Dewey wasn't moving.

"All right, Dewey, out, out, out," Cynthia said, pulling on his behind. "I'd hate for you to lose an eye." Dewey got the message and jumped back, only to start burrowing under the pile of branches on the floor.

"This is going to take all day," Cynthia said.

"I sure hope so," I replied.

As Cynthia pulled the last branches out of the box, I started to assemble the tree. Dewey was prancing and grinning, watching my every move. He came in for a sniff and a taste, then bounced back a few feet. The poor cat looked like he was about to explode with excitement.

Hurry up, hurry up. I want my turn. This was the happiest I'd seen him all year.

"Oh, no, Dewey, not again."

Oh boy, Dewey had buried himself in the Christmas tree box again. This time, he disappeared completely inside, and a few seconds later the box was rolling back and forth across the floor. He stopped, poked his head out, and looked around. He spotted the half-assembled tree and bolted back to chew on the lower branches.

"I think he's found a new toy."

"I think he's found a new *love*," I said as I put the top branches into the notches on the trunk of our tree.

It was true. Dewey loved the Christmas tree. He loved the smell of it. The feel of it. The taste of it. Once I had it assembled and set up next to the circulation desk, he loved to sit under it. *Mine now*, he said as he rounded the base a few times. *Just leave us, thanks.*

"Sorry, Dewey. Still work to do. We don't even have it decorated yet."

Out came the ornaments: new tinsel, angels on strings, Santa Clauses, ribbons, bells, shiny balls with glitter all over them. One minute Dewey was crawling around in the boxes, finding out which ornaments came next. The next minute he was at our feet, playing with our shoelaces. Then he was stretching into the tree for another whiff of plastic. A few seconds later he was gone.

"What's that rustling sound?"

Suddenly Dewey came tearing by us with his head caught in one of the plastic grocery bags we used for storage. He ran all the way to the far side of the library, then came careening back toward us.

"Catch him!"

Dewey dodged and kept running, his head still caught in the bag. Soon he was on his way back. Cynthia blocked the area near the front door. I took the circulation desk. Dewey sprinted right between us. I could see from the look in his eyes he was in a frenzy. He had no idea how to get the plastic bag from around his neck. His only thought was, *Keep running. Maybe I can lose this monster.*

Soon there were four or five of us chasing him, but he wouldn't stop dodging and sprinting away. It didn't help that we were all laughing at him.

"Sorry, Dewey, but you've got to admit this is funny."

I finally cornered him and, despite his terrified squirming, managed to free him from the bag. Relieved, Dewey immediately went over to his new best friend, the Christmas tree, and lay down under the branches for a nice, comforting tongue bath. There would be a hair ball, no doubt, but at least a lesson had been learned: No plastic bags for the Dew.

The next step, now that the Christmas tree was up, was gifts. Every year, the librarians received a few gifts from grateful patrons. Eventually, they made a nice little stack of chocolates and cookies.

But our stack was dwarfed by Dewey's enormous pile of balls, treats, and toy mice. There were some fancy toys, even some nice homemade items, but Dewey's favorite new plaything wasn't a gift at all; it was some red yarn he found in a decorating box. That ball of yarn quickly became Dewey's constant companion.

He batted it around the library until a few feet of yarn stuck out, which he then pounced on, wrestled, and, very soon, got wrapped around his body. More than once, I was almost run down by an orange cat streaking across the library, red yarn around his legs and the bundle dragging behind him. An hour later, he'd be sacked out under the Christmas tree, all four feet clutching his big red buddy.

The library closed for three days on Christmas Eve, so Dewey came home with me. We spent Christmas morning together. I didn't give him a present, though. After a year together, our relationship was well beyond token gifts. We didn't have anything to prove.

All Dewey wanted from me was a few hours a day of my time. I felt the same way. So, that was what we gave each other—on our first Christmas and on every one that followed.

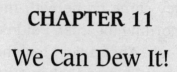

CHAPTER 11

We Can Dew It!

When I was growing up on a farm in Iowa, I thought the town of Moneta was big. It only had five hundred people, but it had a gas station, a dance hall, a restaurant, and a general store where kids would stand transfixed in front of a giant counter full of penny candies and whistles. There was a wonderful school and a baseball field. We even had bees. A local family had sixty hives and their honey was famous in four counties, which seemed like the whole wide world.

But do you know what happened to Moneta? It disappeared. Not closed down, I mean *gone,* like most of the buildings just got up and walked away. There's still a turnoff where the pavement turns into a dirt road, but there isn't a town. Not really. There are maybe ten houses, but there isn't a single open business. More than half the buildings on the old downtown strip from my childhood are gone, torn down to make way for a cornfield.

Even my farm is gone. We couldn't afford to keep it, so my dad sold it to our neighbor. That neighbor leveled our farmhouse, chopped down our trees, and turned the entire 160 acres into farmland. He even straightened our creek. I can drive by now without even recognizing it. The first four feet of our dirt driveway is all that remains of my childhood.

It's like that in Iowa. It's a great life, but it's also hard. Out here, there are rolling hills, but no mountains. There are rivers and creeks, but only a few lakes up in the county north of Spencer. The wind has worn down the rock outcroppings, turning them first to dust, then dirt, then soil. There's not much out here but fine black farm-land and long straight roads. And if something goes wrong, there aren't many ways to fix it. If the processing plant burns down, or the crops fail, or the bank goes under, your town could disappear. But we never thought that would happen to Spencer, even though times were tough.

I knew families were suffering. The parents never discussed their problems with me. They probably didn't discuss them with their closest friends. That's not the way they were; we didn't talk about our personal circumstances, be they good, bad, or indifferent. But you could tell.

One boy wore his old coat from the previous winter. His mother stopped wearing her makeup, then her jewelry. The boy loved Dewey; he clung to Dewey like a true friend, and his mother never stopped smiling when she saw them together. Then, around October, the boy and his mother stopped coming to the library. The family, I found out, had moved away.

And they weren't the only ones. In the late 1980s, the population of Spencer dropped from eleven thousand to eight thousand. People were leaving the county, even the state, looking for jobs. And there still weren't enough jobs in Spencer for the people that were left.

But we never lost faith. Do you know why? Because Spencer had been through worse. On June 27, 1931, at 1:36 p.m., an eight-year-old boy lit a sparkler outside Otto Bjornstad's drugstore at

Main and West Fourth Street. Someone screamed, and the startled boy dropped the sparkler into a large display of fireworks. The display exploded. The fire, whipped by a hot wind, spread across the street. Within minutes the blaze was burning down both sides of Grand Avenue. At the height of the blaze, even the pavement caught fire. By the end of the day, thirty-six buildings housing seventy-two businesses, more than half the businesses in town, were destroyed.

Can you imagine what those people thought as they looked at the smoke floating out over the fields and the smoldering remains of their beloved town? That afternoon northwest Iowa must have felt like a lonely place.

But do you know what they did? They started working. Within two days, the businesses were opening in barns and garages. Within a year, most of the buildings on Grand Avenue had been rebuilt bigger and better than ever. Around here, we call that progressive. If something bad happens, you don't complain about it, you use the opportunity to make it better. That's progressive.

And that's what happened during those bad times in the 1980s, back when the stores started closing and Christmas almost had to be canceled.

Instead of complaining, we became "progressive." We started working harder. We built parks; we fixed the sidewalk and streetlights downtown. We rebuilt the best hotel in town, which had fallen into ruin. Guess what we called it? You guessed it, the Hotel.

As library director, I wanted to do my part. My plan was to remodel the library. I knew the library wasn't just a place to keep books; it was a social center of town. A nice library would make everyone feel better. So as soon as I became library director, I started pressing for money to remodel. The city council made all the decisions, so that's where I went...again and again and again.

"Money for the library?" They laughed. "But we already have enough books."

"The library isn't a warehouse," I told them. "It's a community center. We have meeting rooms, story hours, computers. Newly paved roads are nice, but they don't lift our community's spirits. Not like a warm, friendly library. Wouldn't it be great to have a library we're proud of?"

"I got to be honest," they said. "I don't see how prettier books make a difference."

Then a funny thing happened: Dewey changed

everything. I wanted the library to feel more comfortable. Dewey made it feel like a home. I wanted people to come and spend more time at the library. Once Dewey arrived, more people started coming. And they were staying longer, too. They were leaving happier, and that happiness was being carried to their homes, their schools, and their jobs. Even better, people were talking.

"I was down at the library," someone would comment.

"Was Dewey there?"

"Of course."

"Did he sit in your lap? He always sits on my daughter's lap."

"Actually, I was reaching for a book on a high shelf, and instead of a book I accidently grabbed Dewey. I was so startled I dropped a book right on my toe."

"What did Dewey do?"

"He laughed."

"Really?"

"No, but I sure did."

It wasn't a remodel that changed the library; it was a cat! A wonderful, friendly, personable cat who made everyone welcome. That was Dewey's charm: he didn't play favorites. He loved everybody. And everybody loved him in return.

Eventually, even the city council started to notice the change. Slowly, their attitude shifted. They began to realize, thanks to Dewey, that the library was a social center for the town. And they discovered that a good library really could make people happy and proud.

And do you know what? After years of saying no, they finally said yes to the library remodel. And it was all because of Dewey.

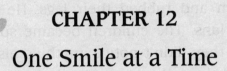

CHAPTER 12

One Smile at a Time

How did Dewey change the library? By changing the people who visited it, of course!

For instance, every week the library hosted a Story Hour for local special education classes. Before Dewey, the kids were poorly behaved. This was their big outing for the week and they were excited: screaming, yelling, jumping up and down. But Dewey changed that. As they got to know him, the children learned that if they were too noisy or erratic, Dewey left. They would do anything to keep Dewey with them; after a few months, they became so calm you couldn't believe it was the same group of kids.

Most of the children were physically limited, so they couldn't pet Dewey very well. Dewey didn't care. As long as the children were quiet, he spent the hour with them. He walked around the room and rubbed their legs. He jumped in their laps. The children became so fixated on him, they didn't notice anything else. If we had read them the phone book they wouldn't have cared.

Crystal was one of the more challenged members of the group. She was a beautiful girl of about eleven, but she had no speech and very little control of her limbs. She was in a wheelchair, and the wheelchair had a wooden tray on the front. When she came into the library, her head was always down and her eyes were staring at that tray. When the teacher took off her coat, she didn't even move. It was like she wasn't there.

Dewey noticed Crystal right away, but they didn't form an immediate bond. She didn't seem interested in him, and there were plenty of children who desperately wanted his attention. Then one week Dewey jumped on Crystal's wheelchair tray. Crystal squealed. She had been coming to the library for years, and I didn't even know she could make noises. That squeal was the first sound I ever heard her make.

After that, Dewey started visiting Crystal every week. Every time he jumped onto her tray, Crystal squealed with delight. It was a loud, high-pitched squeal, but it never scared Dewey. He knew what it meant. He could feel her excitement. Or maybe he could see the change in her face. Whenever she saw Dewey, Crystal glowed. Her eyes had always been blank. Now they were on fire.

Soon it wasn't just seeing Dewey on her tray that got Crystal excited. The moment the teacher pushed her into the library, Crystal was alive. When she saw Dewey, who usually waited for her at the front door, she immediately started to vocalize. It wasn't her usual high-pitched squeal but a deeper sound. I think she was calling to Dewey. Dewey must have thought so, too, because as soon as he heard it, he was at her side. Once her wheelchair was parked, he jumped on her tray, and she was so, so happy. She started to squeal, and her smile, you couldn't believe how big and bright it was. Crystal had the best smile in the world.

Usually Crystal's teacher picked up her hand

and helped her pet Dewey. The feel of his fur on her skin always brought on a round of louder and more delighted squeals. I swear, one day she looked up and made eye contact with me. She was overcome with joy, and she wanted to share the moment with someone. Yes, this was the same girl who for years never lifted her eyes from the floor.

One week I picked Dewey off Crystal's tray and put him inside her coat, which she was wearing half unzipped. She didn't even squeal. She just stared down at him in awe. She was so happy. Dewey was so happy. He had a chest to lean on, and it was warm, and he was with somebody he loved. He wouldn't come out of her coat. He stayed in there for twenty minutes. The other children checked out books. Dewey and Crystal sat together in front of the circulation desk. The bus was idling in front of the library, and all the other children were on it, but Dewey and Crystal were still sitting where we had left them, alone together. That moment was worth the world.

I can't imagine Crystal's life. I don't know how she felt when she was out in the world, or even what she did. But I know that whenever she was in the Spencer Public Library with Dewey, she was happy. And I think she experienced the kind of complete happiness very few of us ever feel. Dewey knew that. He wanted her to experience that happiness, and he loved her for it.

Isn't that a legacy worthy of any cat—or human being?

CHAPTER 13

Dewey's Big Sister

There was another special person Dewey helped as well. Have you guessed who it was? That's right: it was me. I had a great life, I really did, but I'd also had some hard times. I didn't get to go to college; I had to work in a factory. I had health problems. I got divorced at age thirty—and I didn't even know how to drive a car! But maybe the hardest thing of all, if you can believe it, was seeing my daughter Jodi growing up.

When she was young, Jodi was my best friend. We walked our cockapoo, Brandy, together. We went window-shopping at the mall (because we couldn't afford to actually buy anything). We had sleepovers in the living room. *The Wizard of Oz*—over the rainbow where everything is in color and you have the power to do what you've always wanted if only you knew how to tap into it—came on television once a year. There were no video rental stores or DVDs or pay-per-view movies back then, so that was our only chance to see our favorite movie for the year. The night it came on, we would have a picnic and sleepover in front of the television and talk and talk and talk about it all night long.

Even the two-hour drive to my parents' house in Hartley, Iowa, was fun. Jodi and I would laugh and sing along to corny seventies songs by John Denver and Barry Manilow. And we always played a special game. I would say, "Who's the biggest man you know?"

Jodi would answer, and then ask me, "Who's the strongest woman you know?"

I would answer and ask, "Who's the funniest woman you know?"

We asked questions back and forth until eventually I could think of only one more question. "Who's the smartest woman you know?"

Jodi always answered, "You, Mommy." She had no idea how much I looked forward to hearing that.

Then Jodi turned ten. At ten, Jodi stopped answering the question.

At thirteen, we had moved to Spencer. After that, she stopped letting me kiss her good night. "I'm too old for that, Mommy," she said one night.

"I know," I told her. "You're a big girl now." But it broke my heart.

By the time Jodi was sixteen, I felt we were living separate lives. It wasn't her fault; a lot of times, that just happens.

And then came Dewey.

With Dewey, I had something to talk about that Jodi wanted to hear. I'd tell her what he did and who came to see him. The librarians alternated feeding Dewey on Sunday mornings when the library was closed. Although I was never able to get Jodi out of bed for those Sunday morning visits, we'd often drop by the library Sunday night on our way back from dinner at my parents' house.

You wouldn't believe Dewey's excitement when Jodi walked in that library door. The cat pranced. He would do backflips off bookshelves just to impress her.

Dewey never followed anyone around...

except Jodi. He was absolutely crazy about Jodi. Even when Jodi came to the library during work hours, Dewey sprinted to her side. He didn't care who saw him; he had no pride around that girl. As soon as she sat down, Dewey was in her lap.

I always brought Dewey home with me on holidays, when the library was closed for a few days. He spent the first couple of minutes crouched on the floor in the backseat—he always worried we were going to see his veterinarian Dr. Esterly—but as soon as he felt me turn onto Eleventh Street, he bounced up to stare out the window. As soon as I opened the door, he rushed into my house to give everything a nice long sniff. Then he ran up and down the basement stairs about a hundred times. He couldn't get enough of those stairs.

When he finally got tired, Dewey would often settle in beside me on the sofa. Just as often, though, he sat on the back of the sofa and stared out the window. He was watching for Jodi. When she came home, he jumped right up and ran to the door. As soon as she walked in, Dewey was Velcro.

He never left Jodi's side. He ran between her legs and almost tripped her. When she took her shower, he sat in the bathroom and stared at the shower curtain. If she closed the door, he sat right outside. If the shower stopped and she didn't come out quickly enough, he cried. As soon as she sat down, he was on her lap. It didn't matter if she was at the dinner table or on the toilet. He jumped on her, kneaded her stomach, and purred, purred, purred.

Jodi's room was an absolute mess. When it came to her appearance, my daughter was immaculate. Not a hair out of place. Put it this way: she ironed her socks. So who would believe her room looked like the lair of a troll? You couldn't see the floor, crusty plates and glasses were buried under dirty clothes, and the closet was so stuffed with junk you couldn't close the door. I refused to clean up after her, but I also refused to stop nagging her about it. Just like a typical mother, right?

But Dewey didn't care. Dirty room? Nagging mother? *That's Jodi in there,* he said to me with one last look as he disappeared behind her door for the night. *What does that other stuff matter?*

Sometimes, just before turning in for the night, Jodi would call me to her room. I'd walk in and find Dewey guarding Jodi's pillow. Other times, he'd be lying right on top of her face.

"Mmmm," she'd say as he rolled over onto her mouth. "Ah camf breeff."

I'd look at him for a second and then, suddenly…Jodi and I would both start laughing.

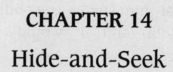

CHAPTER 14

Hide-and-Seek

Have you ever been in a library after closing? Of course not! (Or at least I hope not.) Well, let me tell you: a library after closing is a lonely place. It is very quiet, and the rows of shelves create a lot of dark and creepy corners. Most of the librarians I know won't stay alone in a library after dark. But I worked at the Spencer Public Library almost every night after everyone else had gone home, and I was never scared. I was strong. I was stubborn. And most of all, I was never alone. I had Dewey.

While I worked, Dewey sat on top of my computer screen, lazily swiping his tail back and forth. Type, swipe. Type, swipe. When I stopped, he always jumped down onto the keyboard. *No more,* he'd say. *Let's play.* Dewey had an amazing sense of timing.

"All right, Dewey," I told him. "You go first."

Dewey's game was hide-and-seek, so as soon as I gave the word he would take off around the corner. Half the time I spotted the back half of a long-haired orange cat immediately. To Dewey, hiding meant sticking your head into a bookshelf; he seemed to forget he had a tail.

"I wonder where Dewey is," I said out loud as I snuck up on him. "Boo!" I yelled when I got within a few feet, sending Dewey running.

Other times he was better hidden. I would sneak around a few shelves with no luck, then turn the corner to see him prancing toward me with that big Dewey smile.

You couldn't find me! You couldn't find me!

"That's not fair, Dewey. You only gave me twenty seconds."

Occasionally he curled up in a tight spot and stayed put. I'd look for five minutes, then start calling his name. "Dewey! Dewey!" That dark library could get a little scary, but I always imagined Dewey hiding just a few feet away, laughing at me.

"All right, Dewey, that's enough. You win!"

Nothing. Where could that cat be? Just when I was giving up, I'd turn around and there he was, standing in the middle of the aisle, staring at me.

"Oh, Dewey, you clever boy. Now it's my turn."

I'd run and hide behind a bookshelf, and invariably one of two things happened. I'd get to my hiding place, turn around, and Dewey would be standing right there. He had followed me.

Found you. That was easy.

His other favorite thing to do was run around the other side of the shelf and beat me to my hiding spot.

Oh, is this where you're thinking about hiding? Because, well, I've already figured it out.

I'd laugh and pet him behind the ears. "Fine, Dewey. Let's just run for a while."

We'd run between the shelves, meeting at the end of the aisles, nobody quite hiding and no one really seeking. After fifteen minutes I would completely forget my troubles. Whatever had been bothering me, it was gone. The weight, as they say, was lifted.

"Okay, Dewey. Let's get back to work."

Dewey never complained. I'd climb back into my chair, and he'd climb back on top of the computer and start waving his tail in front of the screen. The next time I needed him, he'd be there.

It's not a stretch to say those games of hide-and-seek with Dewey got me through a lot of hard nights. Maybe I should tell you Dewey put his head on my lap and whimpered while I cried, or that he licked the tears from my face. You could understand that, right? And it is almost true, because sometimes when the ceiling started falling in on me and I found myself staring blankly down at my lap, tears in my eyes, Dewey was there, right where I needed him to be.

Dewey was a loving cat—he was always a soft touch, for instance, for a late-night cuddle. But he was still a cat, so he liked his personal space. He didn't just bathe me with affection all the time. Somehow, though, he always knew when I needed a little nudge or a warm body, and he knew when the best thing for me was a silly, mindless game of hide-and-seek.

And whatever I needed, he'd give me, without thought, without wanting something in return, and without me asking. It wasn't just love. It was more than that. It was respect. It was empathy. And it went both ways. That connection Dewey and I had felt when we met? Those nights alone together in the library turned it into an unbreakable bond.

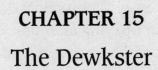

CHAPTER 15

The Dewkster

We started remodeling the Spencer Public Library in the spring, just as northwest Iowa was waking up and changing from brown to green. The lawns suddenly needed mowing, and the trees on Grand Avenue were throwing out new leaves. On the farms, the plants were pushing through the soil, and you could finally see the result of all that time spent fixing equipment, churning fields, and planting seeds. The weather turned warm. The kids brought out bicycles. At the library, after a year of planning, it was finally time to get to work.

The first step was painting the bare concrete walls. Tony Joy, our painter and the husband of staff member Sharon Joy, threw some drop cloths over the books and leaned his ladder against the shelves. Easy, right? But as soon as his ladder went in, Dewey climbed up.

"All right, Dewey," Tony said. "Down you go."

Dewey wasn't paying attention. He'd been in the library more than a year, but he'd never seen it from nine feet up. With a few steps along the top of the bookshelves, he was out of reach.

Tony moved the ladder. Dewey moved again. Tony climbed to the top of the ladder, propped his elbow on the bookshelf, and looked at this stubborn cat.

"This is a bad idea, Dewey. I'm going to paint this wall, then you're going to rub against it. Vicki's going to see a blue cat, and then you know what's going to happen? I'm going to get fired."

Dewey just stared.

"You don't care, do you?"

I wasn't worried about Dewey. He was the most conscientious cat I'd ever known. He raced down bookshelves without a misstep. He intentionally brushed displays with his side, but never knocked them over. I knew he could not only walk on a shelf without touching wet paint, but also tiptoe up a ladder without knocking off the paint can at the top. I was more worried about Tony. It's not easy sharing a ladder with the King of the Library.

"I'll take my chances," Tony joked. "As long as you don't blame me for the big blue cat."

Within a few days, Tony and Dewey were fast friends. Or maybe I should say Tony and Dewkster, because that's what Tony always called him: The Dewkster. Tony felt Dewey was too soft a name for such a macho cat. He worried the local alley cats were assembling outside the library window at night to make fun of his name. So Tony decided his real name wasn't Dewey, it was the Duke. "Only his close friends call him Dewkster," Tony explained.

When Tony finished the painting three weeks later, Dewey was a changed cat. Maybe he thought he really was the Duke, because suddenly he wasn't content with just naps and laps. He wanted to explore. And climb. And most important, explore new places to climb. We called this Dewey's Edmund Hillary phase, after the famous mountain climber. (Sir Edmund Hillary was the first Westerner to climb Mount Everest.) Dewey didn't want to stop climbing until he'd reached the top of his personal Mount Everest, which he managed to do about a month later.

"Any sign of Dewey this morning?" I asked Audrey Wheeler, who was working at the circulation desk. "He didn't come for breakfast."

"I haven't seen him."

"Let me know if you do. I want to make sure he's not sick."

Five minutes later I heard Audrey utter what around here was a surprising profanity: "Oh, my golly!"

She was standing in the middle of the library, looking straight up. And there, on top of the ceiling lights, looking straight down, was Dewey.

When he saw us looking, Dewey pulled his head back. He was instantly invisible. As we watched, Dewey's head reappeared a few feet down the light. Then it disappeared again. Then it appeared a few feet farther on. Dewey had figured out how to climb up on top of the lights. He had clearly been up there for hours, watching us.

"How are we going to get him down?"

"Maybe we should call the city," someone suggested. "They'll send someone with a ladder."

"Let's just wait him out," I said. "He's not doing any harm up there, and he'll have to come down for food eventually."

An hour later Dewey trotted into my office, licking his lips from a late breakfast, and jumped into my lap. He was clearly keyed up about this new game, but didn't want to overplay his hand. I knew he was dying to ask, *What do you think of that?*

"I'm not even going to mention it, Dewey."

He cocked his head at me.

"I'm serious."

Okay then, I'll nap. Exciting morning, you know.

It took a few weeks for us to figure out his method of getting up to the lights. It was pretty ingenious. First, Dewey jumped on an empty computer desk. Then he jumped on a filing cabinet. That gave him a long jump to the top of the temporary wall around the staff area, where he could hide behind a huge quilt of Spencer history. From there, it was only four feet to the lights.

Sure, we could have rearranged the furniture, but once he figured it all out we knew there wasn't much, except old age and creaky bones, that could stop Dewey from walking the lights. When cats don't know something exists, it's easy to keep them away. If they can't get to something they've made up their minds they want, it's almost impossible. Cats aren't lazy; they'll put in the work to thwart even the best-laid plans.

Besides, Dewey loved being up on the lights. He loved walking back and forth from end to end until he found an interesting spot. Then he would lie down, drape his head over the side, and watch. The patrons loved it, too. Sometimes when Dewey was pacing you could see them craning up at the ceiling, their heads going back and forth like clock pendulums. When Dewey was pointed out to the children, his head just peeking over the edge of the lights, they screamed with excitement. They had so many questions.

"What's he doing?"

"How'd he get up there?"

"Why is he up there?"

"Will he get burned?"

"What if he falls off? Will he die?"

"What if he falls on somebody? Will they die?"

When the children found out they couldn't join him on the ceiling, they begged him to come down. "Dewey likes it up there," we explained. "He's playing." Eventually even the children understood that when Dewey was on the lights, he was coming down only on his terms. He had discovered his own little heaven up there.

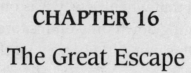

CHAPTER 16

The Great Escape

By August, the remodeling was over. Attendance was up. The staff was happy. Dewey had not only been accepted by the town of Spencer, but people were inspired by him. The Clay County Fair, the biggest event of the year, was just around the corner in September. Everything was perfect—except Dewey. My contented baby boy, our library hero, was a changed cat: distracted, jumpy, and most of all, trouble.

During the remodel, big heavy things were constantly being moved in and out of the library, so Dewey had spent three weeks that summer at my house. Now, late summer is the best time of year in Spencer. The corn is ten feet high, golden and green. The sun is warm. The fields go on and on and on. You leave the windows open, just to catch the scent. It's hard, sometimes, to stay inside.

All day, Dewey stared through my window screens at the world outside. He couldn't see the corn, but he could hear the birds. He could feel the breeze. He could smell whatever cats smell when they direct their noses to the great outdoors.

Now he missed it. There were windows in the library, but they didn't open. You could smell the new carpet but not the outdoors. You could hear the trucks, but not the birds. *How can you show me something so wonderful,* he seemed to whine, *then take it away?*

At the front of the Spencer Public Library was a tiny lobby with glass doors on both sides. For two years Dewey hated that lobby; when he returned from his three weeks at my house, he adored it. From the lobby, he could hear the birds. When the outer doors were open, he could smell fresh air. For a few hours in the afternoon, there was even a patch of sunlight. Dewey loved sunlight! He pretended that was all he wanted, to sit in that patch of sun and listen to the birds.

But we knew better. Dewey really wanted to go through that second set of doors and into the outside world.

"Dewey, get back in here!" a librarian would yell every time he followed a patron into the lobby. The circulation desk faced the lobby; the poor cat had no chance of not being seen. So Dewey stopped listening.

Eventually, the library staff started coming back to get me. I was Mom. Dewey always listened to me. Or at least he used to. Now I had to resort to more serious methods.

"Dewey, do you want me to get the bottle?" I'd say when he refused to come out of the lobby.

He'd just stared at me.

I'd bring the squirt bottle, which Dewey hated as much as his baths, out from behind my back. With the other arm, I'd hold open the door to the library. Dewey would slink back inside.

Ten minutes later: "Vicki, Dewey's in the lobby again!"

Finally, I'd had enough. No more Mrs. Nice Mom. I stormed out of my office, used my best Mom voice, threw open the lobby door, and demanded, "You get in here right now, young man."

Unfortunately, a real young man was sitting in the lobby, and he almost jumped out of his skin when the crazy lady started yelling. Before the last word was out of my mouth, he had rushed into the library, grabbed a magazine, and buried his head in it all the way up to the fine print. Talk about embarrassing. I was holding the door open in stunned silence, unable to believe I hadn't seen this guy right in front of my face, when Dewey came trotting past like nothing had happened. I could almost see him smiling.

A week later, I couldn't find Dewey anywhere. Nothing unusual there; Dewey had plenty of places to hide. There was a cubbyhole behind the display case by the front door that was about the size of a box of crayons. There was the brown lounge chair in the children's area, although his tail usually stuck out of that one. Then there was "between the books." In a library, books fit on both sides of a shelf. Between the two rows is about four inches of space. "Between the books" was Dewey's ultimate hiding place. The only way to find him was to lift books and look behind them. That doesn't sound so difficult until you consider that the Spencer Public Library contained more than four hundred shelves of books. Between those books was an enormous labyrinth, a long, narrow world all Dewey's own.

Fortunately he almost always stuck to his favorite place: the bottom row of Westerns. Not this time. He wasn't under the brown lounger, either, or in his cubbyhole. I didn't notice him peeking down from the lights. I opened the doors to the bathrooms to see if he had been locked inside. Not this morning.

"Has anyone seen Dewey?"

No. No. No. No.

"Who locked up last night?"

"I did," Joy said, "and he was definitely here." I knew Joy would never have forgotten to look for Dewey. She was the only librarian, besides me, who would stay late with him to play hide-and-seek.

"Good. He must be in the building. Looks like he's found a new hiding place."

But when I returned from lunch, Dewey was still missing. And he hadn't touched his food. That's when I began to worry.

"Where's Dewey?" a patron asked.

We had already heard that question twenty times. I told the staff, "Tell them Dewey's not feeling well. No need to alarm anyone." He'd show up. I knew it.

That night, I drove around for half an hour instead of heading straight home. I wasn't expecting to see a fluffy orange cat prowling the neighborhood, but you never know. The thought going through my mind was, *What if he's hurt? What if he needs me, and I can't find him? I'm letting him down.* I knew he hadn't run away. But...

He wasn't waiting for me at the front door the next day. I stepped inside and the place felt dead. A cold dread walked up my spine, even though it was ninety degrees outside. I knew something was wrong.

I told the staff, "Look everywhere."

We checked every corner. We opened every cabinet and drawer. We pulled books off the shelves, hoping to find him in his crawl space. We shined a flashlight behind the wall shelves. Some of them had pulled an inch or two away from the wall; Dewey could have been making his rounds, fallen in, and gotten stuck. Clumsiness wasn't like him, but in an emergency you check every possibility.

The night janitor! The thought hit me like

a rock, and I picked up the phone. "Hi, Virgil, it's Vicki at the library. Did you see Dewey last night?"

"Who?"

"Dewey. The cat."

"Nope. Didn't see him."

"Is there anything he could have gotten into that made him sick? Cleaning solution maybe?"

He hesitated. "Don't think so."

I didn't want to ask, but I had to. "Do you ever leave any doors open?"

He really hesitated this time. "I prop open the back door when I take out the garbage."

"How long?"

"Maybe five minutes."

"Did you prop it open two nights ago?"

"I prop it open every night."

My heart sank. That was it. Dewey would never just run out an open door, but if he had a week to think about it, peek around the corner, sniff the air . . .

"Do you think he ran out?" Virgil asked.

"Yes, Virgil, I do."

We set up shifts so that two people could cover the library while the rest of us looked for Dewey. The regular patrons could tell something was wrong. "Where's Dewey?" went from an innocent inquiry to an expression of concern. We continued to tell most patrons nothing was wrong, but we took the regulars aside and told them Dewey was missing. Soon a dozen people were walking the sidewalks. *Look at all these people. Look at all this love. We'll find him now,* I told myself again and again.

I was wrong.

I spent my lunch hour walking the streets, looking for my baby boy. He was so sheltered in the library. He wasn't a fighter. He was a finicky eater. How was he going to survive?

On the kindness of strangers, I thought. Dewey trusted people. He wouldn't hesitate to ask for help.

I dropped in on Mr. Fonley at Fonley Flowers, which had a back entrance off the alley behind the library. He hadn't seen Dewey. Neither had Rick Krebsbach at the photo studio. I called all the veterinarians in town. We didn't have an animal shelter, so a vet's office was the place someone would take him. I told the vets, "If someone brings in a cat who looks like Dewey, it probably is Dewey. We think he's escaped."

I told myself, *Everyone knows Dewey. Everyone*

loves Dewey. If someone finds him, they'll bring him back to the library.

I didn't want to spread the news that he was missing. Dewey had so many children who loved him, not to mention the special needs students. Oh, my goodness, what about his friend Crystal? I didn't want to scare them. I knew Dewey was coming back.

When Dewey wasn't waiting for me at the front door on the third morning, my stomach plummeted. I realized that, in my heart, I had been expecting to see him sitting there. When he wasn't, I was devastated. That's when it hit me: Dewey was gone. He probably wasn't coming back. I knew Dewey was important, but only at that moment did I realize how big a hole he would leave. To the town of Spencer, Dewey *was* the library. How could we go on without him? How could I go on without him?

The mood in the library was black. Yesterday we had hope. We believed it was only a matter of time. Now we believed he was gone. We continued to search, but we had looked everywhere. I sat down and thought about what I was going to tell the community. I would call the radio station. They would immediately make an announcement. They could mention an orange cat without saying his name. The adults would understand; maybe they could keep it from the children for a while.

"Vicki!"

Then the newspaper. They would run the story tomorrow. Maybe someone had taken him in.

"Vicki!"

Should we put up flyers? What about a reward?

"Vicki!"

Who was I kidding? He was gone. If he was here, we would have found—

"Vicki! Guess who's home!"

I stuck my head out of the office and there he was, my big orange buddy, wrapped in the arms of Jean Hollis Clark. I rushed over and hugged him. He laid his head on my chest.

"Oh, baby boy, baby boy. Don't ever do that again."

Dewey didn't need me to tell him. I could tell this was no joke. Dewey was purring like he had on our first morning. He was so happy to see me, so thankful to be in my arms. But I knew him so well. Underneath, in his bones, he was still shaking.

"I found him under a car on Grand Avenue," Jean was saying. "I was going over to White Drug, and I happened to catch a glimpse of orange out of the corner of my eye."

I wasn't listening. I would hear the story many times over the next few days, but at that moment I wasn't listening. I only had eyes and ears for Dewey.

"He was hunched against the wheel under a car. I called to him, but he didn't come. He looked like he wanted to run, but he was too afraid. He must have been right there all along. Can you believe that? All those people looking for him, and he was right there all along."

The rest of the staff was crowding around us now. I could tell they wanted to cuddle him, but I didn't want to let him go.

"He needs to eat," I told them. Someone put out a fresh can of food, and we all watched while Dewey sucked it down. I doubt he had eaten in days.

Once he had done his business—food, water, litter box—I let the staff hold him. He was passed from hand to hand like a hero in a victory parade. When everyone had welcomed him home, we took him out to show the public. Most of them didn't know anything had happened, but there were a few wet eyes.

That afternoon I gave Dewey a bath, which he tolerated for the first time since that cold January morning so long ago. He was covered in motor oil, which took months to work out of his long fur. He had a tear in one ear and a scratch on his nose. I cleaned them gently.

Was it another cat? A loose wire? The undercarriage of a car? I rubbed his cut ear between my fingers, and Dewey didn't even flinch. "What happened out there?" I wanted to ask him, but the two of us had already come to an understanding. We would never talk about this incident again.

Years later, I would make it a habit to prop open a door during library board meetings. Cathy Greiner, a board member, asked me every time, "Aren't you worried Dewey will run out?"

I looked down at Dewey, who was always there to attend the meeting. He looked up at me. That look told me, as clearly as if he'd crossed his heart and hoped to die, that he wasn't going to run. Why couldn't everyone else see it?

"He's not going anywhere," I told her. "He's committed to the library."

And he was. For sixteen years, Dewey never went into the lobby again. He lounged by the door, especially in the morning, but he never followed patrons out. If the doors opened and he heard trucks, he sprinted to the staff area. He didn't want to be anywhere near a passing truck. Dewey was completely done with the outdoors. He was really and truly a library cat.

THE DAILY ROUTINE

7:30 A.M.
Mom arrives. Demand food, but don't be too hasty. Watch everything she does. Follow at her heels. Make her feel special.

8:00 A.M.
Staff arrives. Spend an hour checking in with everyone. Find out who is having a tough morning and give her the honor of petting me for as long as she wants. Or until ...

8:58 A.M.
Prep time. Take up position by the front door, ready for first patron of the day. This also has the added benefit of alerting distracted staff of current time. I hate it when they open late.

9:00–10:30 A.M.
Doors open. Greet patrons. Follow the nice ones, but give everyone a chance to brighten their day by paying attention to me. Petting me is a gift for visiting the library.

10:30 A.M.
Find lap for nap. Laps are for naps, not playing. Playing in laps is for kittens.

11:30–11:45 A.M.
Lounge. Middle of Adult Nonfiction, head up, paws crossed in front. The humans call this the Buddha pose. I call it the Lion King. *Hakuna matata.* No, I don't know what it means, but the kids keep talking about it.

11:45 A.M.–12:15 P.M.
Sprawl. When it gets too tiring to hold head up, assume the sprawl: full out on back, paws sticking out in four directions. Petting is assured. But don't fall asleep. Fall asleep, and you're vulnerable to a belly wrestle attack. I hate belly wrestle attacks.

12:15–12:30 P.M.

Lunch in the staff room. Anybody got yogurt? No? Then never mind.

12:30–1:00 P.M.

Cart ride! When the clerks shelve books, jump on the cart and hitch a ride around the library. Oh, man, it's relaxing to go completely limp and let my legs hang down between the bars of the metal rack.

1:00–3:45 P.M.

Afternoon free time. See how the day is going. Mix in a trip up to the lights with more lap time. Greet the afternoon crowd. Spend ten minutes with Mom. Fur licking is encouraged, not mandatory. And don't forget to find a nice box to nap in. As if it's possible to forget that!

3:55 P.M.

Dinner. They keep thinking dinnertime is four o'clock. If I sit here long enough, they'll learn.

5:05 P.M.

Mom leaves. Jump around so she'll remember I want to play. A running jump off a bookshelf, complete with somersault, works every time.

5:30 P.M.

Play. Mom calls it Boodha Track because that's what the letters on the side say. I guess that's the "real name." I call it the Ball Thingy because there's nothing better than batting that ball around that track. Except for playing with my red yarn. I absolutely love my red yarn. Does anyone want to dangle it for me?

9:05 P.M.

Last shift leaves. Repeat 5:05 routine, but don't expect the same results unless Joy's working the night shift. Joy always finds time to wad up paper and toss it across the library. Sprint after the paper as fast as possible, but once I get there, always ignore it.

9:10 P.M.–7:30 A.M.

My time! None of your business, nosy!

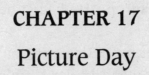

CHAPTER 17

Picture Day

About two months after Dewey's escape, I took him for his first official photograph. I'd like to say it was for sentimental reasons, or that I realized Dewey was on the cusp of something far bigger than either of us ever imagined, but the real reason was a coupon. Rick Krebsbach, the town photographer, was offering pet photographs for ten dollars.

Dewey was such an easygoing cat that I convinced myself that having a professional portrait taken, in a professional portrait studio, would be easy. But Dewey hated the studio. As soon as we walked in, his head was swiveling around, his eyes staring at everything. I put him in the chair, and he immediately hopped out. I picked him up and put him in the chair again. I took one step back, and Dewey was gone.

"He's nervous," I said as I watched Dewey sniff the photo backdrop. "He hasn't been out of the library much."

"That's nothing," Rick said as we watched Dewey dig his head under a pillow. "One dog tried to bite my camera. Another dog actually ate my fake flowers. Now that I think about it, he puked on that pillow."

I quickly picked up Dewey. He was still looking around, more nervous than interested.

"There's been quite a bit of, um...unfortunate peeing," Rick said. "I had to throw away a sheet. To an animal like Dewey, it must smell like a zoo."

"He's not used to other animals," I said. The truth, though, was that Dewey never cared about other animals. He always ignored the Seeing Eye dog who came into the library. He even ignored the Dalmatian that stared through the window at him almost every day. This wasn't fear; it was confusion.

"He knows what's expected of him in the library, but he doesn't understand this place."

"Take your time."

A thought. "May I show Dewey the camera?"

"If you think it will help."

Dewey posed for photographs at the library all the time, but those were personal cameras. Rick's camera was a large professional model. Dewey had never seen one of those before, but he was a fast learner.

"It's a camera, Dewey. Camera. We're here to get your picture taken."

Dewey sniffed the lens. He leaned back and looked at it, then sniffed it again.

I pointed. "Chair. Sit in the chair."

I put him down. He sniffed up and down every leg, and twice on the seat. Then he jumped into the chair and stared right at the camera. Rick hurried over and snapped six photos.

"I can't believe it," he said as Dewey climbed down off the chair.

I didn't want to tell Rick, but this happened all the time. Dewey always seemed to know what I wanted. Unfortunately that didn't mean he was always going to obey. I didn't even have to say *brush* or *bath*; all I had to do was *think* about them, and Dewey disappeared. I remember passing him in the library one afternoon. He

113

looked up at me with his usual lazy indifference. *Hi, how you doing?*

I thought, *Oh, there are two knots of fur on his neck. I should get the scissors and cut them off.* As soon as the idea formed in my mind, *whoosh*, Dewey was gone.

But since his escape, Dewey had been using his powers for good, not mischief. He not only anticipated what I wanted, he did it. Not when a brushing or a bath was involved, of course, but for library business. That was one reason he was so willing to have his photograph taken. He wanted to do what was best for the library.

"He knows it's for the library," I told Rick, but I could tell he wasn't buying it. Why would a cat care about a library? And how could he connect a library with a photo studio a block away? But it was the truth, and I knew it.

I picked Dewey up and petted his favorite spot, the top of his head between the ears. "He knows what a camera is. He's not afraid of it."

"Has he ever posed before?"

"At least two or three times a week. For visitors. He loves it."

"That doesn't sound like a cat."

I wanted to tell him Dewey wasn't just any cat,

but Rick had been taking pet photographs all week. He'd probably heard it a hundred times already.

And yet if you see Dewey's official photograph, which Rick shot that day (it's on the cover of this book, so stop and look at it if you want), you can tell immediately he's not just another cat. He's beautiful, yes, but more than that, he's relaxed. He has no fear of the camera. His eyes are wide and clear. His fur is perfectly groomed. He doesn't look like a kitten, but he doesn't look like a grown cat, either. He's like a young man getting his high school graduation photograph taken: his posture is remarkably straight, his head cocked, his eyes staring calmly into the future. I smile every time I see that photo because he looks so serious. He looks like he's trying to be strong and handsome but can't quite pull it off because he's so darn cute.

A few days after receiving the finished photographs, I noticed the Spencer Shopko, a large general merchandise store sort of like Wal-Mart, was holding a pet photo contest to raise money for charity. You paid a dollar to vote, and the money was used to fight muscular dystrophy.

On a whim, I entered Dewey in the contest.

The photo was for library promotion, and wasn't this a perfect opportunity to promote this special aspect of the library? A few weeks later, Shopko strung a dozen photos, all of cats and dogs, on a wire in the front of the store. The town voted, and Dewey won by a landslide. He got more than 80 percent of the votes, seven times as many as the runner-up. It was ridiculous. When the store called to tell me the results, I was almost embarrassed.

Part of the reason Dewey won so overwhelmingly was the beautiful photograph.

Part of the reason was Dewey's looks. He's so handsome you'd have to love him.

Part of the reason was Dewey's personality. Most cats in photographs look scared to death, desperate to pee, disgusted by the whole process—or often all three. Most dogs look like they are about to go absolutely bonkers, knock over everything in the room, get themselves wound up in an electrical cord, and then eat the camera. Dewey looks calm.

But mostly, Dewey trounced the competition because the town had adopted him. Not just the regular library patrons, but the whole town. While I wasn't watching, Dewey had been quietly working his magic. The stories, not just about his rescue but about his life, were seeping down into the cracks and sprouting new life. He wasn't just the library's cat. He was Spencer's cat. He was our inspiration, our friend, our survivor. He was one of us. And at the same time, he belonged to us.

Was he a mascot for Spencer, the way he was for the library? No. But did he make a difference in the way the town thought about itself? Absolutely. Dewey reminded us, once again, that we were a different kind of place. We cared. We valued the small things.

Dewey was one more reason to love this hardy little town on the Iowa plains.

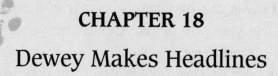

CHAPTER 18

Dewey Makes Headlines

It's amazing: sometimes when you stop running and start relaxing, the world comes to you. Or if not the world, then at least Iowa. Soon after the Shopko contest, Dewey was the subject of Chuck Offenburger's Iowa Boy column in the *Des Moines Register*. Iowa Boy was one of those columns that said things like, "It was the most shocking piece of news I'd come across since the time a few years ago I found out the Cleghorn Public Library, just down the road a ways, had started checking out cake pans to its patrons." Yes, in Iowa, many of the libraries have pans for baking cakes.

When I read the article about Dewey, I thought, *Wow, the Dew's really made it*. It was one thing for a town to adopt a cat. It was even better for a region to adopt that cat, as northwest Iowa had with Dewey. The library received visitors every day from small towns and farms in surrounding counties. Summer residents of the Iowa lake country drove down to meet him, then spread the word to their neighbors and guests, who would drive down the following week. He appeared frequently in the newspapers of nearby towns.

But the *Des Moines Register*! That was the daily newspaper in the state capital. The *Des Moines Register* was read all over the state. More than half a million people were probably reading about Dewey right now. That was more people than attend the Clay County Fair!

After Iowa Boy, Dewey started making regular appearances on our local television newscasts, which originated out of Sioux City, Iowa, and Sioux Falls, South Dakota. Soon he began appearing on stations in other cities and states. Every segment started the same way, with a voice-over: "The Spencer Library wasn't expecting anything more in their drop box than books on a freezing January morning..." No matter how they framed it, the picture was the same. A poor kitten, almost frozen to death, begging for help. The story of Dewey's arrival at the library was irresistible.

But so was his personality. Most news crews weren't used to filming cats—there were thousands of cats in northwest Iowa, no doubt, but few ever made it on television—so they always started out with what seemed like a good idea: "Just have him act natural."

"Well, there he is, sleeping in a box with his tail hanging out and his stomach oozing over the side. That's as natural as it gets."

Five seconds later: "Maybe he can jump or something?"

Dewey always gave them what they wanted. He jumped over the camera for a flying action shot. He walked between two displays to show his dexterity. He ran and jumped off the end of a shelf. He played with a child. He played with his red yarn. He sat quietly on top of the computer and stared into the camera. He wasn't showing off. Posing for the camera was part of Dewey's job as publicity director for the library, so he did it. Enthusiastically!

Dewey's appearance on *Living in Iowa*, an Iowa Public Television series that focuses on issues, events, and people in the state of Iowa, was typical. The *Living in Iowa* crew met me at the library at seven-thirty in the morning. Dewey was ready. He rolled. He jumped between the shelves. He walked up and put his nose on the camera. He stuck right by the side of the beautiful young host, totally winning her over.

"Can I hold him?" she asked.

I showed her the Dewey Carry—over the left shoulder (never the right!), with his behind in the crook of your arm. If you wanted to hold him for any length of time, you had to use the Dewey Carry.

"He's doing it!" the host whispered excitedly as Dewey draped over her shoulder.

Dewey's head popped up. *What did she say?*

"How do I get him to calm down?"

"Just pet him."

The host stroked his back. Dewey lay his head on her shoulder and cuddled against her neck. "He's doing it! He's really doing it! I can feel him purring."

I was tempted to tell her, "Of course he's doing it. He does it for everyone," but why spoil her excitement?

Dewey's episode aired a few months later. It was called "A Tale of Two Kitties." (It's a play on the famous Charles Dickens book *A Tale of Two Cities*.) The other kitty was Tom, who lived in Kibby's Hardware in Conrad, Iowa. Like Dewey, Tom was found on the coldest night of the year.

Store owner Ralph Kibby took the frozen stray to the vet's office. "They gave him sixty dollars' worth of shots," he said on the program, "and said if he's still alive in the morning he may have a chance." As I watched the show, I realized why the host was so happy with Dewey that morning. There were at least thirty seconds of footage of Dewey lying on her shoulder; the best she could get from Tom was a sniff of her finger.

Well, now Dewey was really famous. Pretty soon we had three or four people a week coming into the library to show Dewey off to their friends. "We're here to see the famous cat," an older man said, approaching the desk.

"He's sleeping in the back. I'll go get him."

"Thanks," he said, motioning to a younger woman with a little blond girl hiding behind her leg. "I wanted my granddaughter Lydia to meet him. She's from Kentucky."

When Lydia saw Dewey, she smiled and looked up at her grandfather. "Go ahead, sweetie. Dewey won't bite." The girl tentatively stretched out her hand to Dewey; two minutes later she was stretched out on the floor, petting him.

"See?" her grandfather said to the little girl's mother. "I told you it was worth the trip."

Later, while the mother was petting Dewey with her daughter, the grandfather came up to me and said, "Thanks so much for adopting Dewey." It seemed he wanted to say more, but I think we both understood he had already said enough. Thirty minutes later, as they were leaving, I heard the young woman tell the older man, "You were right, Dad. That was great. I wish we had come by sooner."

"Don't worry, Mommy," the little girl said. "We'll see Dewey next year, too."

BASIC RULES FOR CATS WHO HAVE A LIBRARY TO RUN

(ACCORDING TO DEWEY READMORE BOOKS)
FIRST PRINTED IN THE LIBRARY CAT SOCIETY NEWSLETTER,
AND SINCE REPRINTED NUMEROUS TIMES AROUND THE WORLD.

1 STAFF: If you are feeling particularly lonely and wanting more attention from the staff, sit on whatever papers, project, or computer they happen to be working on at the time—but sit with your back to the person and act aloof, so as not to appear too needy. Also, be sure to continually rub against the leg of the staff person who is wearing dark brown, blue, or black for maximum effect.

2 PATRONS: No matter how long the patron plans on staying at the library, climb into their briefcase or book bag for a long comfortable sleep until they must dump you out on the table in order to leave.

3 LADDERS: Never miss an opportunity to climb on ladders. It does not matter which human is on the ladder. It only matters that you get to the top and stay there.

4 CLOSING TIME: Wait until ten minutes before closing time to get up from your nap. Just as the staff is getting ready to turn out the lights and lock the door, do all your cutest tricks in an effort to get them to stay and play with you. (Although this doesn't work very often, sometimes they can't resist giving in to one short game of hide-and-seek.)

BOXES: Your humans must realize that all boxes that enter the library are yours. It doesn't matter how large, how small, or how full the box should be, it is yours! If you cannot fit your entire body into the box, then use whatever part of your body fits to assume ownership for nap time. (I have used one or two paws, my head, or even just my tail to gain entry, and each works equally well for a truly restful sleep.)

MEETINGS: No matter the group, timing, or subject matter, if there is a meeting scheduled in the meeting room, you have an obligation to attend. If they have shut you out by closing the door, cry pitifully until they let you in or until someone opens the door to use the restroom or get a drink of water. After you gain entry, be sure to go around the room and greet each attendee. If there is a film or slide show, climb on any table close to the screen, settle in, and watch the film to its conclusion. As the credits roll, feign extreme boredom and leave the meeting before it ends.

And the library cat's golden rule for all time . . .

Never forget, nor let humans forget, that you own the joint!

CHAPTER 19

Dewey Goes Batty

When Dewey was six, the Spencer Public Library received a technology update. Out went the catalog cards—you've never even heard of those, have you? I admit, they are pretty old-fashioned—and in came the computers. Now, some people think computers are cold, meaning they make you stare at a screen instead of talking to a person. Dewey disagreed. Dewey thought they were warm. Literally. He loved to sit on them and bask in the heat of their exhaust.

Almost as good, at least from Dewey's perspective, were the new sensor posts beside the front door, which beeped if you tried to leave without checking out your library materials. Dewey's new favorite place was just inside the left post. (Just like the left shoulder for the Dewey Carry. Was Dewey left-pawed?) He sat by that post for the first hour of every day, starting promptly at two minutes to nine. And that's where he greeted his friends, including Tony, our painter, who scratched the Dewkster whenever he came by, and Dewey's friend Doris Armstrong, who still brought him little gifts and surprises.

Dewey's friend Crystal moved away, but he still met the special education class every week. He even developed a relationship with Mark Carey, who owned the electronics store on the corner. Dewey knew Mark wasn't a cat lover, and he took fiendish delight in suddenly jumping on the table and scaring him. Mark took delight in bumping Dewey out of whatever chair he was lounging in—chairs were for patrons—even if there was nobody else in the library.

One morning I noticed a businessman in a suit sitting at a table, reading the *Wall Street Journal*. It looked like he had stopped in to kill time before a meeting, so I wasn't expecting to see a fluffy orange tail sticking out at his side. I looked closer and saw that Dewey had plopped down on his newspaper. Busy. Businessman.

Oh, Dewey, I thought, *you're pushing it now.* Then I realized the man was holding the news- paper with his right hand while petting Dewey with his left. One of them was purring; the other was smiling. That's when I knew Dewey had fallen into a comfort zone; nothing in that library could ever bother him.

That's why I was so surprised when I arrived at the library one morning to find Dewey pac- ing. When I opened the door, he ran a few steps, then stopped, waiting for me to follow.

"Do you need to go to the litter, Dewey? You know you don't have to wait for me."

It wasn't the litter, and he didn't have any inter- est in breakfast. He kept pacing back and forth, crying for me. Dewey never cried unless he was in pain, but I knew Dewey. He wasn't in pain.

I tried fixing his food. Nope. I checked to see if he had poop stuck in his fur. Poop in his fur drove him absolutely nuts—and there was no such thing as cat toilet paper. I checked his nose to see if he had a temperature, and his ears to see if he had an infection. Nothing.

"Let's make the rounds, Dew."

Like all cats, Dewey had hair balls. Whenever it happened, our fanatically neat cat was mortified.

But he had never acted this strangely, so I braced myself for the mother of all hair balls. I worked my way through fiction and nonfiction, checking every corner. But I didn't find anything.

Dewey was waiting for me in the children's section. The poor cat was in knots. But I didn't find anything there, either.

"I'm sorry, Dewey. I don't understand what you're trying to tell me."

When the staff arrived, I told them to keep an eye on Dewey. I was busy, and I couldn't spend all morning playing charades with a cat. If Dewey was still acting strangely in a few hours, I would take him to see Dr. Esterly.

Two minutes after the library opened, Jackie Shugars came back to my office. "You're not going to believe this, Vicki, but Dewey just peed on the cards."

I jumped up. "It can't be!"

To check out a book, we still stamped two cards. One went home with you in the book; the other went into a big bin with hundreds of other cards. When you returned the book, we pulled the corresponding card out of the bin and put the book back on the shelf. Sure enough, Dewey had peed in the front right corner of the bin.

I wasn't mad at Dewey. I was worried. He'd been in the library for years; he'd never acted out. This was completely out of character. But I didn't have long to think before one of our regular patrons came up and whispered in my ear, "You better get down here, Vicki. There's a bat in the children's section."

Sure enough, there it was: a bat, hanging by his heels behind a ceiling beam. And there was Dewey at *my* heels.

I tried to tell you. I tried to tell you. Now look what you've done. We could have taken care of this before anyone arrived. Now there are children in the library. I thought you were protecting them!

Have you ever been lectured by a cat? It's not a pleasant experience. Especially when the cat is right.

And especially when a bat is involved. I hate bats. I couldn't stand the thought of having one in the library, and I couldn't imagine being trapped all night with that thing flying all over the place. Poor Dewey.

"Don't worry, Dewey. Bats sleep during the day. He won't hurt anybody."

Dewey didn't look convinced, but I couldn't

worry about that now. I didn't want to scare the patrons, especially the children, so I quietly called the city janitor and told him, "Get down to the library right away. And bring your ladder."

He climbed up for a look. "It's a bat, all right."

"Shhh. Keep your voice down."

He climbed down. "You got a vacuum cleaner?"

I shivered. "Don't use the vacuum cleaner."

"How about Tupperware?"

I just stared at him. This was disgusting.

Someone said, "We've got an empty coffee can. It's got a lid."

The ordeal was over in a matter of seconds. The janitor just clapped the can over the bat and the bat was gone. Thank goodness. I mean, I really, really, really hate bats.

Now I had to sort out the mess in the cards.

"This is my fault," I told Jackie, who was still manning the circulation desk.

"I know." Jackie has a droll sense of humor.

"Dewey was trying to warn us. I'll clean this up."

"I figured you would."

I pulled out about twenty cards. Underneath them was a big pile of bat guano. Dewey hadn't just been trying to get my attention; he'd been using his scent to cover the stench of the intruder.

"Oh, Dewey, you must think I'm stupid."

He did. He really thought he was much smarter.

The next morning, Dewey started his sentry phase. Each morning, he sniffed three heating vents. He sniffed each one again after lunch. He knew those vents led somewhere and because of that, something might be able to get in. He had taken it upon himself to use his powerful nose to protect us. *If you can't even figure out there's a bat in the library,* he huffed, *how are you going to take care of all these people?*

I know, Dewey. You're right. I'm sorry. It's a good thing we have you.

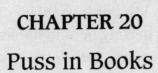

CHAPTER 20

Puss in Books

Meanwhile, while we just went about our regular business in the library, Dewey's fame continued to grow. He was featured in all the cat magazines—*Cats, Cat Fancy, Cats & Kittens*. If the magazine had *cat* in the title, Dewey was probably in it. He even appeared in *Your Cat*, a leading British publication. Marti Attoun, a young freelance writer, traveled to Spencer with a photographer. Her article appeared in *American Profile*, a weekend insert in more than a thousand newspapers. Then, in the summer of 1996, a documentary filmmaker from Boston turned up in out-of-the-way Spencer, Iowa, camera in tow, ready to put Dewey in his first movie.

Gary Roma was traveling the country to create a documentary about library cats. He arrived expecting the kind of footage he'd shot at other libraries: cats darting behind bookshelves, walking away, sleeping, and doing everything possible to avoid looking into the camera. Dewey was exactly the opposite.

He didn't ham it up, but he went about all his usual activities, and he performed them on command. Gary arrived early in the morning to catch Dewey waiting for me at the front door. He shot Dewey sitting by the sensor posts greeting patrons; lying in his Buddha pose; playing with his favorite toys, Marty Mouse and the red yarn; sitting on a patron's shoulder in the Dewey Carry; and sleeping in a box.

Gary said, "This is the best footage I've shot so far. If you don't mind, I'll come back after lunch."

After lunch I sat down for an interview. After a few introductory questions, Gary asked, "What is the meaning of Dewey?"

I told him, "Dewey's great for the library. He

relieves stress. He makes it feel like home. People love him, especially children."

"Yes, but what's the deeper meaning?"

"There is no deeper meaning. Everyone enjoys spending time with Dewey. He makes us happy. What more to life is there than that?"

He kept pressing for meaning, meaning, *meaning*. Gary's first film was *Off the Ground & Off the Wall: A Doorstop Documentary*, and I could imagine him pressing all his subjects: "What does your doorstop mean to you?"

"It keeps the door from hitting the wall."

"Yes, but what about the deeper meaning?"

"Well, I can use it to hold the door open."

"Go deeper."

"Um, it keeps the room drafty?"

About six months after filming, we threw a party for the premiere showing of *Puss in Books*. The library was packed. The movie started with a distant shot of Dewey sitting on the floor of the Spencer library waving his tail slowly back and forth. As the camera zoomed in and followed him under a table, across some shelves, and finally to his favorite book cart for a ride, you heard my voice in the background:

We arrived at work one morning, and we went back to open the book drop and empty the books out, and there inside was this tiny little kitten. He was buried under tons of books, the book drop was just full of books. People will come in, and they'll hear the story of how we acquired Dewey, and they'll say, "Oh, you poor little thing. You were thrown into that book drop on that day.' And I'll say, 'Poor little thing, my foot. That was the luckiest day of that boy's life, because he's king around here, and he knows it."

As the last words rolled out, Dewey stared right into the camera, and boy, could you tell I was right. He really was the king.

By this time, I was used to strange calls about Dewey. The library was getting a couple of requests a week for interviews, and articles about our famous cat were turning up in our mail on an almost weekly basis. Dewey's official photograph (the one on the cover of this book) had appeared in magazines, newsletters, books, and newspapers from Minneapolis, Minnesota, to Jerusalem, Israel. It even appeared in a cat calendar; Dewey was Mr. January. But even I was surprised to receive a phone call from the Iowa office of a national pet food company.

"We've been watching Dewey," they said, "and we're impressed."

Who wouldn't be?

"He seems like an extraordinary cat. And obviously people love him."

You don't say!

"We'd like to use him in a print advertising campaign. We can't offer money, but we will provide free cat food for life."

I have to admit, I was tempted. Dewey was a finicky eater, and we were indulgent parents. We were throwing out dishes full of food every day just because he didn't like the smell, and we were donating a hundred cans of out-of-favor cat food a year. Most of the money for that food was coming out of my pocket. I was personally subsidizing the feeding of a good portion of the cats in Spencer.

"I'll talk to the library board," I said.

"We'll send over samples," the company replied.

By the time the next library board meeting rolled around, the decision had already been made. Not by me or the board, but by Dewey. Mr. Finicky completely rejected the free samples.

Are you kidding me? he told me with a disdainful sniff. *I can't work for this junk.*

"I'm sorry," I told the manufacturer. "Dewey only eats Fancy Feast."

CHAPTER 21

King of the Litter

D ewey's pickiness wasn't just a matter of personality. He had a disease. No, really, it's true. As digestive systems go, that poor cat really got a lemon. Even when he was a kitten, Dewey hated being petted on the stomach. Stroke his back, scratch his ears, even pull his tail and poke him in the eye, but never pet his stomach. I didn't think much of it until Dr. Esterly tried to clean his back end when he was about two years old. "I'll just push down on the glands and squeeze them clean," he explained. "It will take thirty seconds."

Sounded easy enough. I held Dewey while Dr. Esterly prepared his equipment: a pair of rubber gloves and a paper towel. "Nothing to it, Dewey," I whispered. "It will be over before you know it."

But as soon as Dr. Esterly pressed down, Dewey screamed. This wasn't a mild complaint. This was a full-fledged, terrified cry. His body bolted like it had been hit by lightning, and his legs scrambled frantically. Then he threw his mouth over my finger and bit down. Hard.

Dr. Esterly looked at my finger. "He shouldn't have done that."

I rubbed the sore. "It's not a problem."

"Yes, it is a problem. A cat shouldn't bite like that."

I wasn't worried. That wasn't Dewey. I knew Dewey; he wasn't a biter. And I could still see the panic in the poor cat's eyes. He wasn't looking at anything. He was just staring. The pain had been blinding.

After that, Dewey truly hated Dr. Esterly. As soon as we pulled into the veterinary office's parking lot, he started shaking. The smell of the lobby sent him into uncontrollable tremors. He would bury his head in the crook of my arm as if to say, *Protect me.*

As soon as he heard Dr. Esterly's voice, Dewey

growled. Many cats hate the veterinarian in his office but treat him as any other human in the outside world. Not Dewey. He feared Dr. Esterly unconditionally. If he heard his voice in the library, Dewey growled and sprinted to the other side of the room. If Dr. Esterly managed to sneak up on him and reached out to pet him, Dewey sprang up, looked around in panic, and bolted away. I think he recognized Dr. Esterly's smell. Dewey had found his archenemy, and it happened to be one of the nicest men in town.

A few years later, Dewey started having trouble going to the bathroom. Some days, his litter box would have blood in it. Other days, he came tearing out of the back room like someone had lit a firecracker under his rear end.

Dr. Esterly diagnosed Dewey with constipation. Extreme constipation. "What kind of food does Dewey eat?"

I rolled my eyes. Dewey was the world's worst eater. "He's very picky," I said. "He has a remarkable sense of smell, so he can tell when the food is old or off in some way. Cat food isn't the highest quality, you know. It's just a bunch of leftover parts. So you can't blame him."

Dr. Esterly looked at me like a kindergarten teacher eyeing a parent who had just explained away her child's disruptive behavior.

"He always eats canned food?"

"Yes."

"Good. Does he drink water?"

"Never."

"Never?"

"The cat avoids his water dish like poison."

"More water," Dr. Esterly assured me. "That should clear up the problem."

Thanks, Doc, nothing to it. Except have you ever tried to get a cat to drink water against his will? It's impossible.

I started with gentle coaxing. Dewey turned away in disgust.

I tried bribery. "No food until you drink some water. Don't look at me like that. I can last longer than you can." But I couldn't. I always gave in.

I started petting Dewey as he ate. Slowly the petting turned to pushing. *If I force his head down into the water,* I thought, *he has to drink.* Needless to say, that plan didn't work.

Maybe it was the water. We tried warm water. We tried cold water. We tried refreshing the water every five minutes. We tried different faucets.

(Back then, there was no such thing as bottled water in Spencer, Iowa.) We tried putting ice in the water dish. Everyone likes ice water, right? Actually, the ice worked. Dewey took a lick. One lick. But otherwise, nothing. How could an animal stay alive without water?

Then one day I rounded the corner into the staff bathroom. There was Dewey, sitting on the toilet with his head completely buried in the bowl. All I could see was his rear end sticking straight up in the air. Toilet water! He was drinking toilet water! You sly cat!

Well, I thought, *at least he isn't going to get dehydrated.*

But that didn't help his constipation. Even though he drank toilet water, Dewey still couldn't go. When it got really bad, Dewey tended to hide. One morning, poor Sharon Joy reached into the top drawer of the circulation desk for a tissue, but instead grabbed a handful of hair. She literally fell out of her chair.

"How did he get in there?" she asked, staring down at Dewey's back. His head and rear were completely buried in the drawer.

Good question. The drawer hadn't been opened all morning, so Dewey must have climbed in during the night. I poked around under the desk. Sure enough, there was a small opening behind the drawers. But this was the top drawer, more than three feet off the ground. Mr. Rubber Spine had wiggled his way to the top of the crevice, turned a tight corner, and then curled up to sleep in a space no bigger than a cupcake.

I tried to wake him. Dewey shrugged me off and didn't move. This wasn't like him. Obviously something was wrong. Off to the vet's office!

It turns out Dewey had a disease. (See, I told you.) It was called megacolon, and it was extremely rare. If Dewey had lived in the alley, his disease would have shortened his life. In the library, I could expect periodic but severe bouts of constipation, accompanied by very picky eating. So now Dewey had an excuse for not liking his food. That cat had it all figured out, didn't he?

Dr. Esterly suggested an expensive cat food, the kind you could buy only from a veterinarian. I forget the name, maybe Middle-aged Cat with Tummy Troubles Formula? The bill almost broke the budget. I hated to dish out thirty dollars for something I knew wasn't going to work.

I told Dr. Esterly, "Dewey's not going to like this."

"Put it in his bowl. Don't give him anything else. He'll eat it. No cat will starve itself to death."

I put the fancy new food in the bowl, just like Dr. Esterly said. Dewey didn't eat it, just like I thought. He sniffed it once and walked away.

This food, it's no good. I want the usual, please.

The next day, he dropped the subtle approach. Instead of sniffing and walking away, he sat down by the food bowl and cried.

Whhhyyyy? What have I done to deserve this?

"Sorry, Dewey. Doctor's orders."

After two days, he was weak, but he wouldn't even bat the food with his paw. That's when I realized Dewey was stubborn. He was a mellow cat. He was accommodating. But when it came to an important principle like food, Dewey would never roll over and play dog.

And neither would I. Mom could be stubborn, too.

So Dewey went behind my back. First he hit up Sharon Joy by jumping on her desk and rubbing her arm.

When that didn't work, he tried his old friend Joy. Then he tried Audrey, Cynthia, Paula, every librarian, right down the line. He tried Kay, even though he knew she was the no-nonsense type.

Kay was a farm girl, and she had no time for weakness. But I could see even she was beginning to waver. She tried to act tough, but she was developing a real warm spot in her heart for the Dew.

I didn't care. Let them disapprove. I was going to win this round. It might break my heart now, but in the end Dewey would thank me. And besides, I was Mommy, and I said so!

On the fourth day, even the patrons turned on me. "Just feed him, Vicki! He's so hungry." Dewey had been shamelessly putting on a starving cat act for his fans, and it was clearly working.

Finally, on the fifth day, I caved and gave Dewey his favorite can of Fancy Feast. He gobbled it down without even coming up for air. *That's it,* he said, licking his lips and then stepping to the corner for a long tongue bath of his face and ears. *We all feel better now, don't we?*

That night I went out and bought him an armful of cans. I couldn't fight anymore. *Better a constipated cat,* I thought, *than a starving one.*

For two months Dewey was happy. I was happy. All was right with the world.

Then Dewey decided he didn't like Fancy Feast, chunky chicken flavor. He wasn't going to eat another bite of Fancy Feast, chunky chicken flavor. He wanted something new, thank you very much. I bought a new flavor, something in the moist smelly blob category. Dewey took one sniff and walked away. *Nope, not that one, either.*

"You'll eat it, young man, or no dessert for you."

At the end of the day, the food was still there, dried out and crusty. What was I supposed to do? The cat was sick! It took five tries, but I found a flavor he liked. It only lasted a few weeks. Then he wanted something new. Oh boy. The Library King was really getting fussy now!

Soon, the situation was completely absurd. How could you not laugh at an entire bookshelf full of cat food? I'm not exaggerating. We kept Dewey's items on two shelves in the staff area, and one of them was only for food. We had at least five flavors on hand at all times. The Dew had Midwestern taste. His favorite flavors were beef, chunky chicken, beef and liver, and turkey, but you never knew when another flavor would strike his fancy. He hated seafood, but he fell in love with shrimp. For a week. Then he wouldn't touch it.

Even worse, Dewey was still constipated, so on Dr. Esterly's orders I copied a page out of a calendar and hung it on the wall. Every time someone found a present in Dewey's litter box, they marked the date. The calendar was known throughout the office as Dewey's Poop Chart.

When Dewey hadn't gone for three days, we locked him in the back closet with his litter. Dewey hated being locked anywhere, especially a closet.

"It's for your own good, Dew."

After a half hour, I let him out. If no evidence turned up in the litter box, I locked him in for another half hour. No poop, back in the box. Three times was the limit. After three times, he wasn't holding out; he really couldn't go.

This strategy completely backfired. Dewey soon became so pampered he refused to use the litter unless someone took him to the box. He stopped going completely at night, which meant first thing in the morning I had to carry him—yes, carry him—to his litter.

Talk about being the king!

CHAPTER 22

Dewey's Gift

I know, I know. I was a sucker. A spoiler of cats. You should never get in the habit of carrying your cat to the litter box like I carried Dewey. Because if you do, they are going to expect to be carried to their litter every day for the rest of their life.

But Dewey...well, Dewey was a little different. Yes, he expected to be carried, but he gave me something in return. Something I really needed.

You see, about the same time as Dewey's Poop Chart, I got really sick. So sick I worried that I might not be able to work at the library anymore. Everybody knew I was sick, but nobody knew the extent of my pain: not my parents, my friends, not even my daughter, Jodi. The only person that seemed to understand, in his way, was Dewey.

Whenever I had needed him in the past, Dewey had always been by my side. He had perched on my computer at night in the lonely library, and he had sat beside me on the sofa and waited for Jodi. Now he moved from sitting beside me to sitting on my lap. He stopped walking beside me and started insisting on climbing into my arms. That might seem like a small thing, but it made all the difference to me because, you see, I didn't have anybody to touch. There was no one to hug me, to tell me it was going to be okay.

For two years, Dewey touched me every day. He put his head on me. He snuggled in my arms. He seemed to understand that love was constant, but that it could be raised to a higher level when it really mattered.

Every morning since his first week in the library, Dewey had waited for me at the front door. He would stare at me, then turn and run for his food bowl when I opened the door. Then, as I said, he started wanting to be carried to his litter box. And then, on one of the worst mornings of that terrible two years, he did something else: he started waving.

Yes, waving. He was standing at the front door to the library waving.

I stopped and looked at him. He stopped and looked at me. Then he started waving again.

It happened the next morning, too. And the next. And the next, until finally I understood this was our new routine. For the rest of his life, as soon as Dewey saw my car pull into the parking lot, he started scratching his left paw on the front door. The wave continued as I crossed the street and approached the door.

It wasn't frantic. He wasn't meowing or pacing. He was sitting very still and waving at me, as if welcoming me to the library and, at the same time, reminding me he was there. As if I could ever forget. Every morning, Dewey waving at me as I walked toward the library made me feel better: about the job, about life, about myself. If Dewey was waving, everything was all right.

"Good morning, Dewey," I would say, with a smile on my face, even on the darkest and coldest mornings. He would rub against my ankle. My buddy. My boy. Then I would cradle him in my arms and carry him to his litter box like a king. Yes, I was a spoiler of cats. But how could I deny him that?

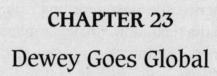

CHAPTER 23

Dewey Goes Global

Of course, I wasn't the only one smitten with King Dewey. As part of my job, I taught courses to other librarians remotely, using a web camera and a videoconferencing system. Every time I sat down to teach the opening class of a course, the first question was, "Where's Dewey?"

"Yes," another librarian would pipe up, "can we see him?"

Fortunately, Dewey attended all meetings at the Spencer Public Library. He preferred meetings of actual people, of course, but teleconferences were acceptable, too. For my courses, he'd lounge in the center of the table waiting for me to push a button and make him appear on viewing screens all over the state. As soon as I did, you could probably hear the gasp in Nebraska.

"He's so cute."

"Do you think my library should get a cat?"

"Only if it's the right cat." That's what I always told them. "You can't get just any cat. He has to be special."

"Special?"

"Calm, patient, dignified, intelligent, and above all, outgoing. A library cat has to love people. It also helps if he's gorgeous and comes with an unforgettable story." I didn't mention that he had to be loving and absolutely love, with his whole heart, being the library cat.

I looked over at my big orange buddy. "You're loving this, aren't you?"

He gave me an innocent look. *Who, me? I'm just doing my job.*

It wasn't just librarians who loved Dewey. I was working in my office one morning when Kay called me to the front desk. Standing there was a family of four, two young parents and their children.

"This nice family," Kay said, "is from Rhode Island. They've come to meet Dewey."

Rhode Island. That was about two thousand miles away!

The father extended his hand. "We were in Minneapolis, so we decided to rent a car and drive down. The kids just love Dewey."

Was this man crazy? Minneapolis was five hours away!

"Wonderful," I said, shaking their hands. "How did you find out about Dewey?"

"We read about him in *Cats* magazine. We're cat lovers."

Obviously.

"Okay," I said, because I couldn't think of anything else. "Let's go meet him."

Dewey was, thank goodness, as eager to please as always. He played with the children. He posed for photographs. I showed the little girl the Dewey Carry, and she walked him all around the library on her left shoulder (always the left). I don't know if it was worth the nine-hour round trip, but the family left happy.

"That was weird," Kay said once the family was gone.

"It sure was. I bet that never happens again."

It happened again. And again. And again. And again. They came from Utah, Washington,

Mississippi, California, Maine, and every other corner of the map. Older couples, younger couples, families. I wish I had thought to write down their names, but I didn't. At first it seemed so unlikely that more people would come. So, why bother? By the time we realized the Dew's appeal, the visitors no longer seemed unusual.

How were these people finding out about Dewey? I had no idea. The library never pursued publicity for Dewey. We never contacted a single newspaper, with the exception of the *Spencer Daily Reporter*. We never hired a publicity agent or marketing manager. After the Shopko cutest pet win, we never entered Dewey in any other contests.

We were Dewey's answering service, nothing more. We just picked up the phone, and there was another magazine, another television program, another radio station wanting an interview. Or we opened the mail and found an article about Dewey from a magazine we'd never heard of or a newspaper halfway across the country. A week later, another family popped up at the library.

Dewey's visitors all left smitten. I know this not only because they told me and because I saw their eyes and their smiles, but because they went home and told people about Dewey. They showed them the pictures. At first they sent letters to friends and relatives. Later, they sent e-mails. He received letters from Taiwan, Holland, South Africa, Norway, Australia. He had pen pals in half a dozen countries. A ripple started in a little town in northwest Iowa, and somehow word of mouth carried it all over the world.

The visitors who truly touched me, though, were the young parents from Texas and their six-year-old daughter. As soon as they entered the library, it was clear this was a special trip for her. Was she sick? Was she sad? Had she lost something? I don't know, but I had the feeling the parents had offered her one wish, and this was it. The girl wanted to meet Dewey. And, I noticed, she had brought a present.

"It's a toy mouse," her father told me. He was smiling, but I could tell he was worried. This was no ordinary spur-of-the-moment visit.

As I smiled back at him, only one thought was going through my mind: "I hope that toy mouse has catnip in it." Dewey would regularly go through periods where he wanted nothing to do with any toy that didn't contain catnip. Unfortunately, this was one of those times.

All I said was, "I'll go get Dewey."

Dewey was asleep in his new fake fur–lined bed, which we kept outside my office door in front of a heating unit. As I woke him up I tried a little mental telepathy: *Please, Dewey, please. This one's important.* He was so tired, he barely opened his eyes.

The little girl was hesitant, as many children are, so the mother petted Dewey first. Dewey lay there like a sack of potatoes. When the girl finally reached out to pet him, Dewey woke up enough to lean into her hand. The father put both Dewey and the girl on his lap. Dewey immediately snuggled up against her.

They sat like that for a minute or two. Finally the girl showed Dewey the present she had brought, carefully tied with a ribbon and bow. Dewey perked up, but I could tell he was still tired. He would have preferred to snooze in the girl's lap all morning. *Come on, Dewey,* I thought. *Snap out of it.* The girl unwrapped the gift, and sure enough, it was a plain toy mouse, no catnip. My heart sank. This was going to be a disaster.

The girl dangled the mouse in front of Dewey's sleepy eyes to get his attention. Then she delicately tossed it a few feet away. As soon as it hit the ground, Dewey jumped on it. He chased that toy; he threw it in the air; he batted it with his paws. The girl giggled with delight. Dewey never played with it again, but while that little girl was here, he loved that mouse. He gave that mouse every ounce of energy he had. And the little girl beamed. She just beamed. She had come hundreds of miles to see a cat, and she was not disappointed. Why did I ever worry about Dewey? He always came through.

DEWEY'S JOB DESCRIPTION

WRITTEN IN RESPONSE TO THE QUESTION, "SO WHAT IS DEWEY'S JOB?",
WHICH WAS OFTEN ASKED AFTER PEOPLE FOUND OUT DEWEY RECEIVED
A 15% LIBRARY EMPLOYEE DISCOUNT FROM DR. ESTERLY.

1 Reducing stress for all humans who pay attention to him.

2 Sitting by the front door every morning at nine to greet the public as they enter the library.

3 Sampling all boxes that enter the library for security problems and comfort level.

4 Attending all meetings in the Round Room as official library ambassador.

5 Providing comic relief for staff and visitors.

6 Climbing in book bags and briefcases while patrons are studying or trying to retrieve needed papers.

7 Generating free national and worldwide publicity for Spencer Public Library. (This entails sitting still for photographs, smiling for the camera, and generally being cute.)

8 Working toward status as world's most finicky cat by refusing all but the most expensive, delectable foods.

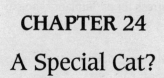

CHAPTER 24

A Special Cat?

I've always wondered: What makes people special? What makes them important?

Often times, it seems, people believe that to be special you have to *do* something—something "in your face" and caught on camera. We like it when a newsworthy town survives a tornado or produces a president. We want an important child to be a star athlete or the smartest kid in the state. And we expect a famous cat to save a child from a burning building, find his way home after being left behind on the other side of the country, or meow "The Star-Spangled Banner."

Dewey wasn't like that. He was like one of those seemingly ordinary people who turn out to be different. He didn't perform spectacular feats. He didn't do one heroic thing; he did something important every single day.

Dewey came from humble beginnings (an Iowa alley); he survived tragedy (a freezing drop box); he found his place (a small-town library). His passion was to make that place, no matter how small and out of the way, a better place for everyone. He spent his time changing lives in Spencer, Iowa, one lap at a time. He never left anyone out, and he never took anyone for granted.

Surely you know Wilbur, the pig in *Charlotte's Web*. Dewey had that personality: enthusiastic, honest, charming, radiant, humble (for a cat), and above all, he was a friend. He wasn't just another cat for people to pet and smile about. Every regular user of the library, *every single one*, felt they had a unique relationship with Dewey.

Like Sharon and Tony's daughter, Emmy, who had Down syndrome and sometimes came on Sunday mornings to see Dewey. Every Saturday night Emmy asked, "Is tomorrow a Dewey day?" The first thing Emmy did every "Dewey day" was search for Dewey. When he was younger, he would usually be waiting by the door, but as he aged, Emmy often found him lying in the sun by a window. She would pick him up and bring him to her mommy so they could pet him together. "Hi, Dewey. I love you," Emmy would say in a soft, kind voice, the way her own mother talked to her. For Emmy, that was the voice of love.

Yvonne Barry, a single woman in her late thirties, came to the library three or four times a week. Every time, Dewey tried to coax her to open the bathroom door for him. Once inside, he'd jump on the sink and beg for the water to be turned on.

He didn't drink this water. He watched it. Something about the way it bounced off the drain plug fascinated him. He'd stare at that water, then suddenly take a quick slap at it with his paw. Watch, watch, watch…slap. Watch, watch, watch…slap. Yvonne would wait for him to finish, then open the door so he could leave. It was their ritual.

But on the day Yvonne had to put her own cat to sleep, Dewey sat with her for more than two hours without asking for a thing. He didn't know what had happened, but he knew something was wrong. Years later, when she told me that story, I could tell it was still important to her.

This is not to say everyone knew Dewey. No matter how famous and popular Dewey became, there was always someone with no idea the Spencer Public Library had a cat. A family would drive from Nebraska to see Dewey. They would bring gifts, spend two hours playing with him and taking pictures. Ten minutes after they left, someone would come up to the desk, obviously worried, and whisper, "I don't want to alarm you, but there's a cat in the library."

"I know," we would whisper back. "He lives here. He's the world's most famous library cat."

"Oh," they'd say with a smile. "Then I guess you already know."

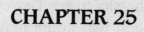

CHAPTER 25

Home Is Where
the Books Are

It wasn't until he turned thirteen years old—
about seventy in human years—that I noticed
for the first time the Dew was mellowing. He
spent more time in his cat bed, and strenu-
ous play was replaced by quiet book cart rides.
Instead of jumping onto the cart, he would meow
for us to pick him up so he could ride at the front
of the cart like the captain of a ship. He stopped
jumping to the ceiling lights, more out of boredom, I believe, than physical necessity.

When Dewey gave up walking the top of the
bookcases, Kay took his old cat bed and put it
on a shelf above her desk. Dewey would snuggle
up in that bed and watch Kay work. One day not
too long after Kay set up the new arrangement,

Dewey jumped up to his bed and the shelf collapsed. The cat flew one way, four legs flailing. Notepads and paper clips flew the other. Before the last paper clip had hit the floor, Dewey was back to survey the damage.

"Not scared of too much in this library, are you?" Kay joked with a smile.

Only the brush and the bath, Dewey would have said if he was being honest. The older Dewey got, the more he hated being brushed and bathed.

He also didn't have as much patience for preschool children, who tended to poke and pull at him. He had always loved children, and he always would, but their roughness was getting harder and harder on his old bones. He was stiffening up, and he could no longer tolerate the small knocks and bruises. He never lashed out at children, and he rarely ran from them. He simply began to scoot away and hide when certain children came looking for him.

Babies were a different story. One day I watched Dewey plop himself down a few feet from an infant girl who was on the floor in a baby carrier. For a full minute, Dewey just sat with a bored expression, looking off into the distance as if to say, *Just happened to be walking by.* Then, when he thought I wasn't looking, he squirmed an inch closer. *Just adjusting my position,* his body language said, *nothing to see here.* A minute later, he did it again. Then again.

Slowly, inch by inch, he crept closer, until finally he was pressed right up against the carrier. He popped his head over the edge, as if to confirm the child was inside. The infant reached her little hand over the edge and snatched his ear. Dewey adjusted his head so she could get a better grip. She laughed, kicking her legs and squeezing his ear. And boy, did she squeeze. Hard. Dewey sat quietly, a contented look on his face.

He was never one to judge. That was one of the best things about Dewey. When he was a kitten, he spent time each day with a homeless woman who came in to pet him. As an older cat, one of his best friends was a homeless man who started appearing at the library every day. The man was unshaven, uncombed, and unwashed. He never said a word to anyone. He never looked at anyone. It was clear he wanted only one thing: Dewey. He would pick Dewey up and drape him over his left shoulder; Dewey would lie there, purring, for twenty minutes, while the man patted him gently.

Our new assistant children's librarian, Donna Stanford, had recently returned to northwest Iowa and didn't know anyone in town. The only local resident who reached out to Donna was Dewey. He loved to ride on her shoulder while she rolled around in her office chair shelving books. When he tired of that, he would climb down onto her lap so Donna could pet him. Sometimes she read him children's books. I caught them by surprise one day, Dewey resting with his eyes closed, Donna deep in thought. I could tell she was startled.

"Don't worry," I said. "It is part of your job description to hold the kitty."

Then there was my daughter Jodi's boyfriend, Scott. The first time he came to Spencer, Jodi and I took Scott to the library to meet Dewey. That's when I knew this relationship was serious; Jodi had never introduced Dewey to one of her boyfriends before.

Dewey was overjoyed to see Jodi. He may have been old, but he still did backflips for that girl! Scott gave the two of them time together, then gently picked Dewey up and petted him. Not on the stomach, which Dewey hated, but along the back. He walked him around the empty library in the Dewey Carry. He pulled out his camera and took a snapshot for his mother. She had heard the Dewey stories, and she was a big fan. Seeing Scott with Dewey, and Dewey with Scott, told me everything I needed to know.

It never occurred to me there was anything unusual about my grown daughter taking her boyfriend to the library to meet her mother's cat. After all, Dewey was more special to me than any animal I had ever known. He was more special to me than I ever believed an animal could be. We had chosen to live our lives together, he and I, not just tomorrow, but forever.

Dewey the cat was part of my family; his opinion mattered. How could anyone seriously consider being a part of this family without knowing him? But all those feelings didn't change a fundamental truth: Dewey belonged in the library. His place was with the public.

Dewey was happy at my house for a day or two whenever it was a holiday, but as soon as we got in the car and headed downtown to the library...oh boy, that cat came alive. He'd put his front feet on the dashboard and stare out the window. I had to take the turns slowly, or he'd slide right off and fall face first on the floor. He was almost shaking with anticipation.

When he smelled Sister's Café, Dewey knew we were a few blocks away. That's when he got really excited. He'd move to the armrest and put his paws on the side window, like he was trying to push the door open. *We're here! We're here!* He'd look over his shoulder and practically yell it to me when we entered the alley. As soon as the door opened, he jumped into my arms and I carried him across the threshold.

And then . . . bliss.

There was nothing Dewey loved more than being home.

CHAPTER 26

Hello Kitty

We received the e-mail in early 2003, when Dewey was fifteen. I had to read it twice, just to make sure. Yes, it was true. Japanese Public Television wanted to film Dewey! They were planning a documentary, and they had discovered Dewey through a feature in the Japanese magazine *Nekobiyori*. Would we mind if a film crew came to Spencer for a day?

That's funny, we had no idea Dewey had appeared in a Japanese magazine!

A few months later, six people from Tokyo, Japan, arrived at the Spencer Public Library. They had flown to Des Moines, rented a van, and driven to Spencer. Iowa in May is beautiful. The corn is just below eye level, three or four feet tall, so you can see the fields spreading into the distance. Of course, it's two hundred miles from Des Moines to Spencer, and that's all you can see. What were six people from Tokyo thinking after three and a half hours of looking at corn? We'd have to ask them, because they were probably the only people from Tokyo ever to make that drive.

The crew had one day to film, so they asked me to arrive at the library before seven. It was a miserably rainy morning. The interpreter, the only woman in the group, asked me to open the first set of doors so they could set up their cameras in the lobby. As they were carting equipment, around the corner came Dewey. He was half-asleep, stretching his back legs as cats often do when they first wake up. When he saw me, he trotted over and gave me a wave. *Oh, it's you. What are you doing here so early? I wasn't expecting you for twenty minutes.* You could have set your watch by that cat.

Once the crew set up the cameras, the interpreter said, "We'd like him to wave again."

Oh, brother. I tried to explain, as best I could, that Dewey waved only once, when he saw me first thing in the morning. The director, Mr. Hoshi, wouldn't hear of it. He was used to not only giving orders but to having them obeyed. He was definitely the man in charge. And right now, he wanted that wave.

So I went back to my car and approached the library again, pretending I hadn't been in that morning. Dewey just stared at me.

What? You were just here five minutes ago.

I entered the library, turned on the lights, turned off the lights, went back to the car, waited five minutes, and approached the library again. Mr. Hoshi thought this might fool Dewey into thinking it was the next day.

It didn't.

We tried for an hour to get footage of Dewey waving. Finally I said, "Look, the poor cat has been sitting there this whole time waiting for his food. I have to feed him." Mr. Hoshi agreed. I scooped Dewey up and rushed to the litter box. The last thing I wanted the Japanese to get on film was flying poop. Dewey relieved himself, then ate a leisurely breakfast. By the time he was finished, the camera crew was set up inside. They had come halfway around the world, and they never got their wave.

But they got everything else. Dewey was slowing down, but he hadn't lost his enthusiasm for strangers. Especially strangers with cameras. He greeted each member of the crew with a rub on the leg; one cameraman even laid his camera on the floor for a Dewey-eye view. Then the interpreter politely asked me to put Dewey on a bookshelf. He sat there and let them film. He jumped from shelf to shelf. Then she said, "Have him walk down the shelf between the books and jump off the end."

I thought, *Wait a second. He's a cat, not a trained animal in the circus, and that's a pretty specific request. I hope you didn't come all this way expecting a show because there's no way he's going to walk that shelf, slalom between the display books, and jump off at command.*

I trudged down to the far end of the shelf and called, "Come here, Dewey." Dewey walked down the shelf, squeezed between the books, and jumped down to my feet.

Amazing.

Anything else? Oh yes, much more. For five hours Mr. Hoshi gave orders and Dewey complied. He sat on a computer. He sat on a table. He sat on the floor with his feet crossed and stared into the camera. He rode on his favorite book cart with his feet hanging down through the openings, completely relaxed. No time to dally; move, move, move.

A three-year-old girl and her mother agreed to appear in the film, so I put Dewey on the glider chair with them. The girl was nervous, grabbing and pulling at Dewey. Dewey didn't mind. He sat through the whole five-minute ordeal and never forgot to stare sweetly at the camera.

I had told the interpreter that people came from all over the United States to visit Dewey, but I don't think Mr. Hoshi believed me. Then, just after lunch, in walked a family from New Hampshire. Talk about timing! The family was at a wedding in Des Moines and decided to rent a car and drive up to see Dewey. Again, that's a three-and-a-half-hour drive!

Mr. Hoshi interviewed the visitors. He took footage of them shooting their own footage of Dewey with their camcorder. I taught the girl, who was five or six, the Dewey Carry, and how to gently rock back and forth until he put his head down on her back and closed his eyes. The family stayed an hour; the Japanese crew left soon after. As soon as they were gone, Dewey fell asleep and was out the rest of the day.

We received two copies of the DVD. The electronics store on the corner loaned us a giant television, and we packed the library for a special viewing. By this time, Dewey had been on the radio in Canada and New Zealand. He had appeared in newspapers and magazines in dozens of countries. His photograph had been all over the world. But this was different. This was worldwide television!

I had sneaked a peek at the video, so I was a little nervous. The documentary was an alphabetic trip through the world of cats. There were twenty-six featured cats, one for each letter of the alphabet. Yes, our alphabet, even though the documentary was in Japanese. Weird, right?

I told the audience, "There are a lot of other cats in this documentary. Dewey is near the end, and the whole thing is in Japanese, so let's take a vote. Should we fast-forward to Dewey's part or watch the whole thing?"

"Watch the whole thing! Watch the whole thing!"

Ten minutes later the crowd was shouting, "Fast-forward! Fast-forward!" Let's just say it was extremely boring to watch cats sitting around and interviews we couldn't understand.

When we hit the letter *W*, a cry went up around the room, no doubt waking the snoozers. There was our Dewey, along with the words *Working Cat* in English and Japanese. There I was, walking up to the library in the rain, while the announcer said something in Japanese. We understood only three words: "America, Iowa-shun, Spencer." Another loud cheer. A few seconds later we heard: "Dewey a-Deedamore Booksa!"

And there was Dewey, sitting at the front door (I have to admit, a wave would have been nice), followed by Dewey sitting on a bookshelf, Dewey walking through two bookshelves, Dewey sitting, and sitting, and sitting and being petted by a little boy under a table and...sitting. One and a half minutes, and it was over. No little girl with Dewey on her lap. No riding the shoulder. No book cart. No family from New Hampshire. They didn't even use the shot of Dewey walking on top of the bookshelf, squeezing between the books, and jumping off the end. They came halfway around the world for a minute and a half of sitting.

There was silence in the library. Stunned silence.

And then a huge burst of cheering. Our Dewey was an international star. Here was the proof. So what if we didn't have a clue what the announcer was saying? So what if Dewey's scene was barely longer than a typical commercial break? There was our library. There was our librarian. There was our Dewey. And the announcer definitely said, "America, Iowa-shun, Spencer."

The town of Spencer has never forgotten that Japanese documentary. We have two copies in the library, but nobody ever watches them. *Puss in Books* is much more popular. But the fact that a film crew came from Tokyo to Spencer? That's something we'll never forget. The local radio station and the newspaper both ran long features, and for months people came into the library to talk about it.

"What was the crew like?"

"What did they eat?"

"Where did they go while in town?"

"What else did they film?"

"Can you believe it?"

"Can you believe it?"

"Can you believe it?"

Of course, Spencer residents aren't the only ones who remember that documentary. After it aired, we received several letters from Japan and forty requests for Dewey postcards. Our library website tallies the origin of online visitors, and for years after the documentary aired, Japan was the second most popular country of origin, after the United States.

Somehow, I don't think those Japanese visitors were interested in checking out our books. They were interested in checking out our Dewey.

CHAPTER 27

The Library Lion

I realized Dewey was losing his hearing when he stopped responding to the word *bath*. For years, that word had sent him into a scamper. The staff would be talking, and someone would say, "I had to clean my bathtub last night."

Bam, Dewey was gone. Every time.

"That isn't about you, Dewey!"

But he wasn't listening. Say the word *bath*—or *brush* or *comb* or *scissors* or *doctor* or *vet*—and Dewey disappeared. Especially if Kay or I said them. When I was away on library business or out sick, Kay took care of Dewey. If he needed something, even comfort or love, and I wasn't around, he went to Kay. She may have been distant at first, but after all those years she had become his second mother, the one who loved him but wouldn't tolerate his bad habits. If Kay and I were standing together and even thought the word *water*, Dewey ran.

Then one day someone said *bath* and he didn't run. Hmm. Interesting. I started to watch him more closely. Sure enough, he had stopped running away every time a truck rumbled by in the alley behind the library. The sound of the back door opening used to send him sprinting to sniff the incoming boxes; now, he wasn't moving at all. He wasn't jumping at sudden loud noises, and he wasn't coming as often when patrons called. That, however, might not have had much to do with hearing.

Dewey was seventeen years old—which is like being about eighty-five in human years. He still greeted everyone at the front door. He still searched out laps, but on his own terms. He had arthritis in his back left hip, and jostling him in the wrong place or picking him up the wrong way would cause him to limp away in pain.

More and more in the late morning and afternoon he sat on the circulation desk, where he was protected by staff. He was supremely confident in his beauty and popularity; he knew patrons would come to him. He looked like a lion surveying his kingdom. He even sat like a lion, with his paws crossed in front of him and his back legs tucked underneath, a model of dignity and grace.

The staff started quietly suggesting that patrons be gentle with Dewey. Joy, especially, became very protective of him. She often brought her nieces and nephews to see Dewey, so she knew how rough people could be. "These days," she would tell the patrons, "Dewey prefers a gentle pet on the head."

Even the elementary school children understood Dewey was an old man now, and they were sensitive to his needs. This was his second generation of Spencer children; their parents were the children who had gotten to know Dewey when he was a kitten. Now they were all grown up! And they made sure their kids were well behaved. When the children touched him gently, Dewey would lie against their legs or, if they were sitting on the floor, on their laps. But rough petting often drove him away.

"That's all right, Dew," I'd reassure him. "Whatever you need."

After years of trial and error, we had finally found our finicky cat an acceptable bed. It was small, with white fake fur sides and an electric warmer in the bottom. We kept it in front of the wall heater outside my office. Dewey loved nothing more than lounging in his bed with the heating pad turned all the way up.

In the winter, when the wall heater was on, he would get so warm he had to throw himself over the side and roll around on the floor. His fur was so hot you couldn't even touch it. He would lie on his back for ten minutes with all his legs spread to let the heat out. If a cat could pant, Dewey would have been panting. As soon as he was cool, he climbed back into his bed in front of the heater and started the process all over again.

Heat wasn't Dewey's only indulgence. I may have been a sucker for Dewey's whims, but our assistant children's librarian, Donna, was spoiling him rotten. If Dewey didn't eat his food right away, she heated it in the microwave for him. If he still didn't eat it, she threw it out and opened another can. Donna didn't trust ordinary flavors. Why should Dewey eat gizzards and toes?

Donna drove to Milford, fifteen miles away, because a little store there sold exotic cat food. She bought duck. Dewey was fond of that for a week. She tried lamb, too, but nothing stuck for very long. Donna kept trying new flavor after new flavor and new can after new can.

Despite our best efforts, though, Dewey was thinning down, so at his next checkup Dr. Franck prescribed a series of medicines to fatten him up. That's right, you heard it, Dewey had a new vet. He had outlasted his old nemesis, Dr. Esterly, who had retired and donated his practice to a nonprofit animal advocacy group.

Along with his medicine, Dr. Franck gave me a pill shooter that, theoretically, shot the pills so far down Dewey's throat that he couldn't spit them out. But Dewey was smart. He took his pill so calmly I thought, *Good, we made it. That was easy.* He'd wait five minutes until I stopped watching him. Then he'd sneak behind a shelf somewhere and cough the pill back up. I found little white pills all over the library.

I didn't force Dewey's to take his medicine. He

was eighteen now (which meant about ninety); if he didn't want medicine, he didn't have to take it. Instead, I bought him a container of yogurt and started giving him a lick every day.

That opened the floodgates. Kay started giving him bites of cold cuts out of her sandwiches. Joy started sharing her ham sandwich; pretty soon Dewey was following her to the kitchen whenever he saw her walk through the door with a bag in her hand. One day Sharon left a sandwich unwrapped on her desk. When she came back a minute later, the top slice of bread had been carefully turned over and placed to the side. The bottom slice of bread was sitting exactly where it had been, untouched. But all the meat was gone.

After Thanksgiving 2005, we discovered Dewey loved turkey, so the staff began saving holiday scraps. We tried to freeze them, but he could always tell when the turkey wasn't fresh. Dewey never lost his keen sense of smell. That's one reason I scoffed when Sharon offered Dewey a bite of garlic chicken, her favorite lunch. I told her, "No way Dewey is going to eat garlic. It's too spicy."

He ate every bite. Who was this cat? For eighteen years, Dewey ate nothing but specific brands and flavors of cat food. Now, he'd eat anything.

I thought, *If we can fatten Dewey up on human food, why not? Isn't that better than a pill?*

I bought him braunschweiger, a cold loaf of sliced liver sausage many people around here consider a delicacy. Braunschweiger is about 80 percent pure fat. If anything would fatten Dewey up, it was braunschweiger. He wouldn't touch it.

What Dewey really wanted was Arby's Beef 'n' Cheddar sandwiches. He gobbled them down. Inhaled them. He didn't even chew the beef; he just sucked it in. I don't know what was in those sandwiches, but once he started on Arby's Beef 'n' Cheddar, Dewey's digestion improved. His constipation decreased. He started eating two cans of cat food a day, and because the Arby's food was so salty, he was slurping down a full dish of water as well. He even started using the litter box on his own.

But Dewey didn't have a couple of owners, he had hundreds, and most of them couldn't see the improvements. All they saw was the cat they loved getting thinner and thinner. Dewey never hesitated to play up his condition. He was a real trickster. He would sit on the circulation desk, and whenever someone approached to pet him, he would whine. They always fell for it.

"What's the matter, Dewey?"

He'd lead them toward his food dish. He'd look forlornly at the food, then back at them, and, with his big eyes full of sorrow, drop his head.

"Vicki! Dewey's hungry!"

"He has a can of food in the bowl."

"But he doesn't like it."

"That's his second flavor this morning. I threw the first can away an hour ago."

"But he's crying. Look at him. He just flopped down on the floor."

"We can't just give him cans of food all day."

"What about something else?"

"He ate an Arby's sandwich this morning."

"Look at him. He's so thin. You have to be feed him more."

"Don't worry, we're taking good care of him."

"But he's so thin. Can't you give him something for me?"

I could...except Dewey did the same thing yesterday. And the day before that. And the day before that. In fact, you're the fifth person he's hit with the starving-cat routine today.

Now, how was I going to tell a patron that? I always gave in, which of course just encouraged more bad behavior. I think Dewey enjoyed the taste of food more when he knew I didn't want to give it to him.

Let's call it the taste of victory.

CHAPTER 28

Don't Judge a
Cat by His Fur

As Dewey entered old age, the kindness of Spencer Public Library patrons really began to show. Friends and visitors alike were gentler around him. They talked to him more and were attentive to his needs. Occasionally someone would comment that he looked weak, or thin, or dirty, but I knew they were concerned because they loved him and wanted him to be well.

"What's wrong with his fur?" was probably the most common question.

"Nothing," I told them. "He's just old."

It's true, Dewey's fur had lost much of its luster. It was no longer radiant orange, but a dull copper. It was also increasingly matted, so much so

I couldn't keep up with a simple brushing. I took Dewey to Dr. Franck, who explained that as cats aged, the barbs on their tongues wore down. Even if they licked themselves regularly, they couldn't do an efficient job grooming because there was nothing to separate the fur. Tangles and mats were just another symptom of old age.

"As for these," Dr. Franck said, studying Dewey's clumped back end, "drastic measures are required. I think we better shave."

When she was done, poor Dewey was fuzzy on one end, naked on the other. He looked like he was wearing a big coat and no pants. A few members of the staff laughed when they saw him, because it was a hilarious sight, but they didn't laugh long. The humiliation on Dewey's face stopped that. He hated it. Just hated it.

He walked away very fast for a few steps, then sat down and tried to hide his rear end. Then he got up, walked quickly away, and sat down again. Start, sit. Start, sit. He finally made it back to his bed, buried his head in his paws, and curled up beneath his favorite toy, Marty Mouse. For days, we found him with his top half sticking out into an aisle and his back end hidden in a bookshelf.

But Dewey's health was no laughing matter. The staff didn't talk about it, but I knew they were worried. They didn't want to be responsible if something happened. Dewey was my cat, and everyone knew it. The last thing they wanted was to have the life of my cat in their hands.

"Don't worry," I told them. "Just do what you think is best for Dewey."

I often traveled out of town on library business. I couldn't promise the staff nothing would happen while I was away, but I told them, "I know this cat. I know when he is healthy, a little sick, and really sick. If he's really sick, trust me, he's going to the vet. I'll do whatever it takes."

Besides, Dewey wasn't sick. He still jumped up and down from the circulation desk, so I knew his arthritis wasn't too bad. His digestion was better than ever. And he still loved company. But it took patience to care for an elderly cat, and frankly, some of the staff didn't think that was their job.

Slowly, as Dewey aged, his support peeled away: first those in town who didn't really like him; then some of the fence-sitters; then a few patrons who only wanted an attractive, active cat; and finally the staff members who didn't want the burden of an elderly cat.

That doesn't mean I wasn't blindsided by the October library board meeting. I was expecting a typical discussion of the state of the library, but the meeting soon turned into a referendum on Dewey. A patron had mentioned he wasn't looking well. Perhaps, the board suggested, we should get him some medical help?

"At his recent checkup," I told them, "Dr. Franck discovered hyperthyroidism. It's just another symptom of age, like his arthritis, his dry skin, and the black age spots on his lips and gums. Dr. Franck prescribed a medication. I rub it in his ear. Dewey has really perked up. And don't worry," I reminded them, "we're paying for the medicine with donations and my own money. Not a single penny of city money is ever spent on Dewey's care."

"Is hyperthyroidism serious?"

"Yes, but it's treatable."

"Will this medicine help his fur?"

"Dullness isn't a disease, it's a function of age, like gray hair on a human." They should understand. There wasn't a head in the room without a few gray hairs.

"What about his weight?"

I explained his diet, from the obsessiveness with which Donna and I changed his cat food to the Arby's Beef 'n' Cheddar sandwiches.

"But he doesn't look good," someone said.

They kept coming back to that. Dewey didn't look good. Dewey was hurting the image of the library. I knew they meant well, but I couldn't understand their thinking. It was true, Dewey didn't look as appealing. Everybody ages. Eighty-year-olds don't look like twenty-year-olds, and they shouldn't. But maybe older people, and older cats, have something to teach us, especially about ourselves.

"Why don't you take Dewey home to live with you? I know he visits you on holidays."

I had thought of that. But I knew Dewey could never be happy living at my house. I was gone too much, and he hated to be alone. He was a public cat. He needed people around him to be happy.

"We've had complaints, Vicki, don't you understand? Our job is to speak for the citizens of this town."

The board seemed ready to say the town didn't want Dewey anymore. I knew that was ridiculous because I saw the community's love for Dewey every day. Maybe the board had received a few complaints, but there had always been complaints. Now, with Dewey not looking his best, the voices were louder. But that didn't mean the town had turned on Dewey. One thing I'd learned over the years was that the people who loved Dewey, who really wanted and needed him, weren't the ones with the loudest voices. They were often the ones with no voices at all.

And even if what the board thought was true, even if the majority of the town had turned its back on Dewey, didn't we nonetheless have the duty to stand by him? Even if only five people cared, wasn't that enough? Even if nobody cared, Dewey loved the town of Spencer. He would always love Spencer. He needed us. We couldn't just toss him out because looking at him, older and weaker, no longer made us proud.

There was another message from the board, too, and it came through loud and clear: Dewey is not your cat. He's the town's cat. We speak for the town, so it's our decision. We know what's best.

I won't argue one fact. Dewey was Spencer's cat. But he was also *my* cat. And finally, in the end, Dewey was *a* cat. At that meeting, I real-ized that in many people's minds, Dewey had gone from being a flesh-and-blood animal with thoughts and feelings, to being an object that could be owned. Library board members loved Dewey as a cat, but they still couldn't separate the animal from the symbol.

And I have to admit, there was another thought going through my mind. *I'm getting older. My health isn't the best. Are these people going to throw me out, too?*

"I know I am close to Dewey," I told the board. "Maybe you think I love Dewey too much. Maybe you think my love clouds my judgment. But trust me. I'll know when it's time. I've had animals all my life. I've put them down. It's hard, but I can do it. The very last thing I want, the very last thing, is for Dewey to suffer."

A board meeting can be a freight train, and this one pushed me off to the side like a cow on the tracks. Someone suggested a committee to make decisions about Dewey's future. I knew the people on that committee would mean well. I knew they would take their duty seriously and do what they thought best. But I couldn't let that happen. I just couldn't.

The board was discussing how many people should be on this Dewey Death Watch Committee when one member, Sue Hitchcock, spoke up. "This is ridiculous," she said. "I can't believe we're even discussing this. Vicki has been at the library for twenty-five years. She's been with Dewey for nineteen years. She knows what she's doing. We should all trust Vicki's judgment."

Thank God for Sue Hitchcock. As soon as she spoke, the train jumped the tracks and the board backed off. "Yes, yes," they muttered, "you're right...too soon, too much...if his condition worsens..."

I was devastated. It stung me to the heart that these people had even suggested taking Dewey away from me. And they could have done it. They had the power. But they didn't. Somehow, we had won a victory: for Dewey, for the library, for the town. For me.

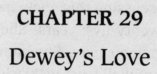

CHAPTER 29

Dewey's Love

In September 2006, just a few weeks before the board meeting where we had talked about Dewey's condition, a program at the library brought in almost a hundred people. I figured Dewey would hide in the staff area, but there he was, mingling as always. He was like a shadow moving among the guests, often unnoticed but somehow there at the end of their hand each time someone reached to pet him. There was a rhythm to his interactions that seemed the most natural and beautiful thing in the world.

After the program, Dewey climbed into his bed above Kay's desk, clearly exhausted. Kay came over and gave him a gentle scratch on the chin. I knew that touch. It was a thank-you, the one you give an old friend after you've watched them across a crowded room and realized how wonderful they are, and how lucky you are to have them in your life. I half expected her to say, "That'll do, cat, that'll do," like the farmer in the movie *Babe*, but Kay left the words unsaid.

Two months later, in early November, Dewey's walk became a bit unsteady. He started peeing excessively, sometimes on the paper outside his litter box, which he had never done before. But he wasn't hiding. He was still jumping up and down from the circulation desk. He still interacted with patrons. He didn't seem to be in pain. I called Dr. Franck, and she advised me just to watch him closely.

Then one morning, just after Thanksgiving, Dewey wasn't waving. All those years, and I could count on one hand the number of times Dewey wasn't waving when I arrived in the morning. Instead he was standing at the front door, just waiting for me. I ushered him to the litter box and gave him his can of cat food. He ate a few bites, then walked with me around the library. I was busy preparing for a trip to Florida, so I left Dewey with the staff for the rest of the morning. As always, he came in while I was working to sniff my air vent and make sure I was safe. The older he got, the more he protected the ones he loved.

At nine-thirty I went out for Dewey's breakfast of the moment, a Hardee's Bacon, Egg and Cheese Biscuit. When I returned, Dewey didn't come running. I figured the deaf old boy didn't hear the door. I found him sleeping on a chair by the circulation desk, so I swung the bag a few times, floating the smell of eggs his way. He flew out of that chair into my office. I put the egg-and-cheese mush on a paper plate, and he ate three or four bites before curling up on my lap.

At ten thirty, Dewey attended Story Hour. As usual, he greeted every child. An eight-year-old girl was sitting on the floor with her legs crossed. Dewey curled up on her legs and went to sleep. She petted him, the other children took turns petting him, everyone was happy. After Story Hour, Dewey crawled into his fur-lined bed in front of the heater, and that's where he was when I left the library at noon. I was going home for lunch, then picking up my dad and driving to Omaha to catch a flight the next morning.

Ten minutes after I got home, the phone rang.

It was Jann, one of our clerks. "Dewey's acting funny."

"What do you mean 'funny'?"

"He's crying and walking funny. And he's trying to hide in the cupboards."

"I'll be right down."

Dewey was hiding under a chair. I picked him up, and he was shaking like the morning I found him. His eyes were big, and I could tell he was in pain. I called the veterinary office. Dr. Franck was out, but her husband, Dr. Beall, was in.

"Come right down," he said.

I wrapped Dewey in his towel. It was a cold day. Dewey snuggled against me immediately.

By the time we arrived at the vet's office, Dewey was down on the floor of my car by the heater, shaking with fear. I cradled him in my arms and held him against my chest. That's when I noticed poop sticking out of his behind.

What a relief! It wasn't serious. It was just poop!

I told Dr. Beall the problem. He took Dewey into the back room to clean him out. Dewey came out wet and cold. He crawled from Dr. Beall's arms into mine and looked up at me with pleading eyes. *Help me.* I could tell something still wasn't right.

Dr. Beall said, "I can feel a mass in his stomach."

"What is it?"

"I don't know. He needs an X-ray."

Ten minutes later, Dr. Beall was back with the results. There was a large tumor in Dewey's stomach, pushing on his kidneys and intestines. That's why he had been peeing more, and it probably accounted for his peeing outside the litter box.

"It wasn't there in September," Dr. Beall said, "which means it's probably an aggressive cancer. But we'd have to do invasive tests to find out for sure."

We stood silently, looking at Dewey. I never suspected the tumor. Never. I knew everything about Dewey, all his thoughts and feelings, but he had kept this one thing hidden from me.

"Is he in pain?"

"Yes, I suspect he is. The mass is growing very fast, so it will only get worse."

"Is there anything you can give him for the pain?"

"No, not really."

I was holding Dewey in my arms, cradling him

like a baby. He hadn't let me carry him that way in sixteen years. Now he wasn't even fighting it. He was just looking at me.

"Do you think he's in constant pain?"

"I can't imagine that he's not."

The conversation was crushing me, flattening me out, making me feel drawn, deflated, tired. I couldn't believe what I was hearing. I had believed Dewey was going to live forever.

I called the library staff and told them Dewey wasn't coming home. Kay was out of town. Joy was off duty. They reached her at Sears, but too late. Several others came down to say good-bye. Instead of going to Dewey, Sharon walked right up and hugged me. Thank you, Sharon, I needed that. Then I hugged Donna and thanked her for loving Dewey so much. Donna was the last to say her good-byes.

Someone said, "I don't know if I want to be here when they put him to sleep."

"That's fine," I said. "I'd rather be alone with him."

Dr. Beall took Dewey into the back room to insert the IV, then brought him back in a fresh blanket and put him in my arms. I talked to Dewey for a few minutes. I told him how much

I loved him, how much he meant to me, how much I didn't want him to suffer. I explained what was happening and why. I rewrapped his blanket to make sure he was comfortable. What more could I offer him than comfort? I cradled him in my arms and rocked back and forth from foot to foot, a habit started when he was a kitten. Dr. Beall gave him the first shot, followed closely by the second.

He said, "I'll check for a heartbeat."

I said, "You don't need to. I can see it in his eyes."

Dewey was gone.

CHAPTER 30

Loving Dewey

For eight days, I didn't read the newspaper. I didn't watch television. I didn't take any phone calls. It was the best possible time to be away in Florida because Dewey's death was hard. Very hard. I broke down on the flight from Omaha and cried all the way to Houston. I cried almost all the way to Florida, too.

Meanwhile, the Spencer radio station devoted their morning show to memories of Dewey. The *Sioux City Journal* ran a lengthy story and obituary. The AP wire picked up the story and sent it around the world. Within hours, news of Dewey's death appeared on the CBS afternoon newsbreak and on MSNBC.

The library started getting calls. If I had been in the library, I would have been stuck answering questions from reporters for days, but nobody else on staff felt comfortable speaking to the media. The library secretary gave a brief statement, which ended up in Dewey's obituary, but that was all. It was enough. Over the next few days, that obituary ran in more than 270 newspapers.

The response from individuals touched by Dewey was equally overwhelming. People in town received calls from friends and relatives all over the country who read about Dewey's death or heard it on a local radio show. One local couple was out of the country and learned the news from a friend in San Francisco, who read about his passing in the *San Francisco Chronicle*.

Admirers set up a vigil in the library. Local businesses sent flowers and gifts. Sharon and Tony's daughter with Down syndrome, Emmy, drew a picture of Dewey. It was two green circles in the middle of the page with lines sticking out in all directions. It was beautiful, and Emmy beamed as I taped it to my office door. That picture was the perfect way for both of us to remember him.

By then, there were letters and cards stacked

four feet high on my desk. I had more than six hundred e-mails about Dewey in my inbox. Many were from people who met him only once but never forgot him. Hundreds of others were from people who never met him.

In the month after his death, I received more than a thousand e-mails about Dewey from all around the world. We heard from a soldier in Iraq who had been touched by Dewey's death despite what he saw there every day—or perhaps because of it. We received a letter from a couple in Connecticut whose son was turning eleven; his birthday wish was to release a balloon to heaven in Dewey's honor.

Many people in town wanted to hold a memorial service. I didn't want a memorial service, but we had to do something. So on a cold Saturday in the middle of December, Dewey's admirers gathered at the library to remember one last time, at least officially, the friend who had had such an impact on their lives. The staff tried to keep it light—I told the story of the bat, Audrey told the story of the lights, Joy remembered the cart rides, Sharon told how Dewey stole the meat out of her sandwich—but despite our best efforts, tears were shed.

Crews from local television stations were filming the event. It was a nice thought, but the cameras seemed out of place. These were private thoughts among friends; we didn't want to share our words with the world. We also realized, as we stood there together, that words couldn't describe our feelings for Dewey. There was no easy way to say how special he was. Finally a local school-teacher said, "People say what's the big deal, he was just a cat. But that's where they're wrong. Dewey was so much more." Everyone knew exactly what she meant.

The next few days were hard. The staff had cleaned out his bowls and donated his food while I was away, but I had to give away his toys. I had to clean out his shelf: the Vaseline for his hair balls, the brush, the red yarn he had played with all his life. I had to park my car and walk to the library every morning without Dewey waving at me from the front door.

When the staff returned to the library after visiting Dewey for the last time, the space heater he had lain in front of every day wasn't working. Dewey had been lying in front of it that very morning, and it had been working fine. It was as if his death had taken away its reason to heat.

Can a malfunctioning piece of equipment break your heart? It was six weeks before I could even think about having that heater repaired.

I had Dewey cremated with one of his favorite toys, Marty Mouse, so he wouldn't be alone. The crematorium offered a free wooden box and bronze plaque, but I didn't want them. Dewey came back to his library in a plain plastic container inside a blue velvet bag. I put the container on a shelf in my office and went back to work.

A week after his memorial service, I came out of my office a half hour before the library opened, long before any patrons arrived, and told Kay, "It's time."

It was December, another brutally cold Iowa morning. Just like Dewey's first morning, and so many in between. It was close to the shortest day of the year, and the sun wasn't yet up. The sky was still deep blue, almost purple, and there was no traffic on the roads. The only sound was the cold wind whipping down the streets and out over the barren cornfields.

We moved some rocks in the little garden in front of the library, looking for a place where the ground wasn't completely frozen. But the whole earth was frosted, and it took a while for Kay to dig the hole. The sun was peeking over the buildings on the far side of the parking lot by the time I placed the remains of my friend in the ground and said simply, "You're always with us, Dewey. This is your home."

Then Kay dropped in the first shovelful of dirt, burying Dewey's ashes forever outside the window of the children's library, at the foot of the beautiful statue of a mother reading a book to her child. As Kay moved the stones back over Dewey's final resting place, I looked up and saw the rest of the library staff in the window, silently watching us.

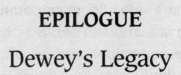

EPILOGUE

Dewey's Legacy

Not much seems to change in northwest Iowa. Spencer has a new mayor, a new drugstore, and a new plastic surgeon, but it's still the same old town. The Spencer Public Library rolls on, even without its library cat. Not that people didn't try to change that fact. After Dewey's death, the library had almost a hundred offers for new cats. We had offers from as far away as Texas. The cats were cute, and most had touching survival stories, but there was no enthusiasm to take one. We couldn't simply replace Dewey with another cat. You can't bring back the past.

Instead, the memories of Dewey live on: At the library, where his portrait hangs beside the front door above a bronze plaque that tells his story;

with the children who knew him and will talk about him with their own children and grand-children; and even in this book. After all, that's why I wrote it. For Dewey.

A few years ago, Spencer commissioned a public art installation to serve as both a state-ment about our values and an entry point to our historic downtown. Two ceramic tile mosaic artists spent a year in the area, talking with us, studying our history, and observing our way of life. More than 570 residents, from young chil-dren to grandparents, consulted with the art-ists. The result is a mosaic sculpture called *The Gathering: Of Time, of Land, of Many Hands.*

The Gathering is composed of four decora-tive pillars and three pictorial walls. The south wall is called "The Story of the Land." It is a farm scene featuring corn and pigs, a woman hanging quilts on a clothesline, and a train. The north wall is "The Story of Outdoor Recreation." It focuses on our parks, the fairgrounds on the northwest edge of town, and the nearby lakes. The west wall is "The Story of Spencer." It shows three generations gathering at Grandma's house, the town battling the fire, and a woman making a pot, a metaphor for shaping the future. Just slightly to the left of center, in the upper half of the scene, is an orange cat sitting on the open pages of a library book. The image is based on artwork submitted by a child.

The story of Spencer. Dewey is a part of it: now and forever.

For me, though, the memories are more personal. I remember the little kitten, so dirty and scared, who I lifted out of the book drop that freezing Monday morning. I remember the way he ate rubber bands. The way he rode on the book cart, with all his feet hanging down. I remember hide-and-seek late at night, the touch of his chin on my arm, and all those mornings he waved at me from the front door and my heart soared right out of my chest with joy.

I remember Dewey's last Christmas. My daughter Jodi and her husband Scott stayed at my house. They had twins, Nathan and Hannah, a year and a half old. Hannah and Nathan would toddle up and pet Dewey all over.

Grandpa Dew was cautious around toddlers. In the library, he slunk away when they tried to approach him. But he sat with the twins, even when they petted him the wrong way and messed up his fur. Hannah kissed him a hundred times;

Nathan accidentally knocked him on the head. One afternoon, Hannah poked Dewey in the face while trying to pet him. Dewey didn't even flinch. This was my grandchild. This was Jodi's child. Dewey loved us, so he loved Hannah, too.

Find your place. Be happy with what you have. Treat everyone well. Live a good life. It isn't about material things; it's about love.

Those are the lessons Dewey taught me. But he also taught me something else: you never know when you'll fall in love.

I had decided, when Dewey died, not to get another cat. I had loved Dewey with all my heart, and he had loved me in the same way. It wouldn't be fair to expect that of another cat. The poor animal would always be compared to Dewey, and how could it possibly compete?

Then, two years later, on another bitterly cold Iowa morning, a friend of mine saw a truck swerve suddenly on an icy road in downtown Spencer. She thought there was a clump of ice or snow in the road, so she slowed down. Then she saw the clump move. It was a scared little kitten, shivering in the cold with ice and twigs matted in its fur. My friend took the kitten to her office and gave him a bath, then brought him to the library.

As soon as I saw the little kitten, my heart leaped. It was like seeing Dewey again that first morning in the library drop box: so tiny, so helpless, so wonderfully, beautifully ginger orange. The new kitten had green eyes instead of Dewey's gorgeous gold, and his tail was stubby and short, but otherwise... he was so much like Dewey. Even his long fur and magnificent ruff of neck hair looked like the Dew.

I picked the kitten up and cradled him in my lap. He looked me in the eye and began to purr. Just like with Dewey that first morning, I melted. This was meant to be. Within an hour, the kitten was on his way to my house to live with me.

That night, I mentioned the new kitten on Dewey's website, www.deweyreadmorebooks.com. I was worried Dewey's fans might be disappointed; after all, they loved him, too. Instead, a boy named Cody wrote back to suggest that, since I was turning a new page in my life, I name the kitten Page.

Cody was right. I was turning a new page in my life. I was moving on, starting a new adventure, writing the first words of a new story in the great big book of my life.

That doesn't mean I will ever forget Dewey. He will always be part of me; he will always live in my heart. But Page Turner (my new cat's full name)...he makes me laugh really, really hard. And when he does that, I know everything in the world is all right.